Andrea Kirshman
1102 Fredrick Blvd.
Reading, PA 19605

Books by
Andrea Van Steenhouse

Empty Nest . . . Full Heart

A Woman's Guide to a Simpler Life

Lifelines: A Personal Journal

Empty Nest...
Full Heart

Empty Nest...
Full Heart

*The Journey from
Home to College*

Andrea
Enjoy the journey
Andrea Van Steenhouse

Andrea Van Steenhouse

Simpler Life Press
Denver, Colorado

Published by Simpler Life Press
222 Milwaukee, Denver, Colorado 80206

Cover illustration and illuminated letters by
Johanna Parker

Cover design and interior layout by Ultimax Inc.,
Denver, Colorado

Printed in the United States of America

VanSteenhouse, Andrea.
Empty Nest . . . Full Heart by Andrea VanSteenhouse

p. cm.

Library of Congress Catalogue
Card Number 97-095131

ISBN 0-9619806-1-3
1 3 5 7 9 10 8 6 4 2
First Edition

To Big Jim and Mother Marge

for the gift of family

Contents

THE CHILD'S APPEAL

I am a child.
All the world waits for my coming.
All the earth watches with interest
To see what I shall become.
The future hangs in the balance,
For what I am,
The world of tomorrow will be.

I am a child.
I have come into your world,
About which I know nothing.
Why I came I know not;
How I came I know not.
I am curious;
I am interested.

I am a child.
You hold in your hand my destiny.
You determine, largely,
Whether I shall succeed or fail.
Give me, I pray you,
Those things that make for happiness.
Train me, I beg you,
That I may be a blessing to the world.

Mamie Cole

Introduction

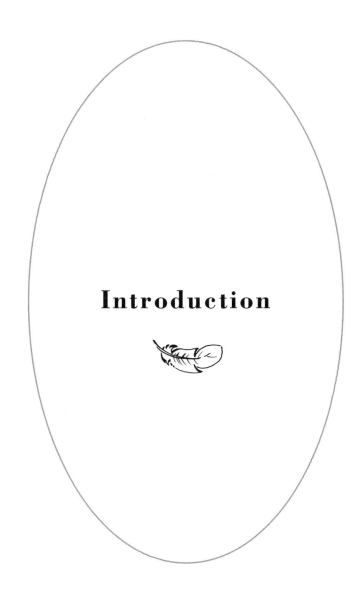

nd so to begin...

It was one of those sparkling amber afternoons of early September when I drove into the parking lot to join my husband for a meeting at the bank. We pulled up next to each other but neither of us made a move to get out of our respective cars. We were each mesmerized by the same National Public Radio commentary in which Donna Damico, a woman who could easily laugh at her family's bumpy route to the fledging of a child, eloquently described the bone-deep sadness she'd experienced when driving her son to college.

Then came the response from her son, who had been listening as he waited his turn to speak. He was already in the excited flush of freshman orientation at his college and keenly ready to begin his new life. Although he was genuinely touched by his mother's feelings, he was eager to be on with the next chapter of his life. It was clear that leaving was easier by far than being left.

The honest, diverging emotions rising from both parts of the interview seemed to fill the car, making it difficult for me to take a breath without having it come out as a slightly embarrassed half-sob. My husband and I, each still in our own car, were emotionally leveled by the conclusion, a passage from Howard Nemerov's poem, "September, The First Day of School."

> *My child and I hold hands on the way to school,*
> *And when I leave him at the first grade door*
> *he cries a little but is brave; he does*
> *let go. My selfish tears remind me how*
> *I cried before that door a life ago.*
> *I may have had a hard time letting go.*

After a poignant description of how the years flew by, the segment ended with a final note of grace from the poem.

> *Even our tears belong to ritual.*
> *But may great kindness come of it in the end.*

I looked over at my husband and saw that he, too, had felt the sweeping fullness of the universal message: children coming of age, families changing ready or not, life going on. We smiled wistfully at each other, haltingly got out of our cars, and went into the meeting still reeling from the potent content of what we had just heard.

I had no son leaving for college. But this was not about leaving–it was about transitions, the cycle of life and the richness of rites of passage. It was for me the touching of a longing for the celebration of rituals and an expression of their power.

It's an odd paradox: With the massive information network we have developed, the heartbeat of life's marker events has been dimmed. It is as if the more we know and can know, the less we're able to embrace the real-time resonance and the harder it is to find and welcome feelings about life's predictable transitions.

One true measure of lives, however, is transcribed in the strong and subtle waves of feeling that etch all of these events upon our psyches. We know we have been there and done it all. These riveting, relentless feelings record and authenticate the various passages of our lives, and even if the dramatic content is quite high at times, it offers us the unequivocal chance to live more deeply, to respond more humanly. Ernest Hemingway once asked: "How will we know it's us without our history?" Our emotional journals won't let us down; we'll know.

Certainly, though, we're busy and we can't watch ourselves live. It is only in moments full of awareness that we are compelled to notice. This heightened awareness calls us out of complacency, lifts us as well to moments which are mentally inscribed for a lifetime, especially events involving our children. How many of us have gasped at something endearing or unique from our offspring, saying silently, "This is too good. I will never forget this moment." Children fill our days. We move from their complete dependency to their pressured independence.

Our goal is to produce loving, competent, responsible adults; the activities which direct us to that end fill our lives as easily as breathing, but the end of our children's dependence brings a wrenching twist. In the

NPR commentary, Ms. Damico complained that she was "being handed early retirement from a job I really like." About preparing to send her first son to college, she went on to say, "I divided my whole world, friends and strangers alike, into two camps—those who looked potentially tearful at my pronouncement and those who didn't."

How can the accomplishment of something so good feel so awful? How is it that when the time has come to let them move on, we beg for just a little more time, only a little longer? Our seasons of mothering and fathering flash before us and seem far too short. Even when the teenage years are trying, letting go is bittersweet. For what could have been. For what will never be. For what was.

The drum beats early for the slow dance to emancipation. The beginning of the senior year launches the journey and marks repeatedly its inevitability. The senior year in every American high school relives the ritually prescribed chronology of events for seniors—the last homecoming game, the senior prom, the yearbook, and finally graduation itself—nudging seniors into emerging adulthood because they have passed through the required forms. The first day of twelfth grade is the last first day of school with us, and so we begin.

That singularly amazing summer following graduation may display the splendor of ambivalence—that of both the parents and the students. It is both respite from the real world of leaving high school and not yet the full flourish of leaving for something else. Perhaps everyone catches an unconscious breath, awaiting what is next with an edgy uncertainty. When it finally comes, the real journey rubs us raw and allows us to feel the intensity of the changing of the guard. Now, there is no turning back.

So many of us feel so full, in concert with others at this transition, yet at the same time we often march toward the end zone in silence. The natural, even eagerly anticipated freedom leaves us feeling saddened, confused, and remarkably alone. It is a common experience with uncommon fervor. It is one that deserves to be chronicled and shared. We can learn from one another's stories and resurrect appreciation of timeless rites of passage, which after all, is appreciation of our human condition.

It is our hope to track this journey with its ample joys and sorrows and to allow for the spirit of change to show its majesty. No one's journey is like our own, yet the spirit of moving on sings a common melody. It is the song of ourselves. It is the memory of our own earlier ritual passage but with a new chorus joined by our offspring merging into the mainstream. Somehow we emerge, but we are different on the other side, as are our children. Rites of passage are supposed to offer this arrival at a new ground more complete than before the experience, and perhaps, though scoured a bit and tested, somewhat wiser.

Stories of those who've recently made the passage instruct us in looking for the lightheartedness, the humor, and even the joy along the way and also leaven for us the denser days with their compassion and their wisdom. These stories and some Home Remedies, offering practical advice for handling each stage of the transition from high school to college, follow in profusion.

Come with us: the journey begins!

I

That

Incomparable

Senior Year

Who has seen the wind?
Neither you nor I...
But when the trees bow down their heads,
The wind is passing by.

⌐ Christina Georgina Rossetti

King of
the Hill

There is something inexplicably different about the first day of school the senior year. Unlike previous years, there is an excitement about this returning that reverberates in a strange new way. A subtle, nuanced difference, but it is as absolute and unmistakable as autumn itself. Somewhat strange and slightly ominous, the day also has the exhilarating sense that things will be very different, and this feeling proves to be the foreshadowing of a year of intensity and drama for everyone. It seems to all begin on this particular first day of school.

For seniors, it's this year alone, after all, that represents the pinnacle of all experience and expectation to this time. It is the provenance and the privilege of twelfth graders to feel entitled, enfranchised, and suffused with a sense of their own power. It happens with the regularity of the school clock announcing the time for the first class. It just universally is.

The seniors expect no less. All tradition which they have witnessed has informed them that this will be true for them as it has for those who came before. The students themselves feel the excitement from the time they can refer to themselves as "seniors" when they finish their last day of their junior year. They can drive, they can make money to spend on play during the summer–they feel as though they have it all. And, from their perspective in their still-protected playing field, they're right!

Our culture has promised them that this exalted position will be theirs at the proper time. For years they have been carefully watching the transmission of power and have seen their own moment coming. Now each in a secular rite of passage, has assumed the role and the mantle of senior class member with the attendant prerogatives afforded the King of the Hill, much like a solemn pageant with everyone in place for the processional.

Of course, the crown for the King of the Hill comes in a variety of sizes. Not everyone wears it so readily or so easily, since not all seniors are that sure they can really take on the world they've been handed.

Those who love high school, in fact, are very lucky. Many others experience it as one long and difficult test. At some point everyone experiences emotional and bodily changes, shifts in friendships, class demands, competition for grades, and brutal peer pressure. The intensity and resolution of each of these issues color the whole experience. Many high school students feel they don't fit and are grateful to be leaving; graduation presents a welcome opportunity to reinvent the self and have a second chance in life. Further, a high school can be a bad fit for a student, just a bad match.

For all the dramas associated with high school, it is at best a complex stretch. Our collective hope is that the challenges of those times of insecurity and tentativeness will give all children the strength and character to greet life's new lessons. High school is a crucible experience by any measure, though, and offers many arenas for challenge, even when they are presented over and over.

As for parents, it's hard to say when they first recognize the senior's budding power emerging from a newly entitled sense of freedom and privilege. Perhaps it's when the senior chooses an easy schedule or no early classes. If registration is right before school begins, as it is for many, there is a quiet decision going on, but it may not be an entirely conscious process. It generally takes about two weeks before the parents realize that the drop/add paper they signed in a moment of weakness has actually permitted all sorts of creative options. It may be rash to refer to an easy schedule as "dramatic avoidance," yet it is just the beginning of the ambivalence and the quest for independence that will be the theme for the whole year.

After waiting for hours in lines for schedule changes, one senior honors student was elated to switch into jewelry making and to a second session of team sports. She explained her "senior concept." She'd excelled for three years and planned the results that would lead to an easy schedule. The plan included time for clubs, sports, and "off" periods. Her parents' patient urging regarding the importance of more academic subjects for the college application process fell on deaf ears. Finally, the parents retreated to hoping for high grades in the "senior concept" classes for college acceptance.

The combinations of emotions and the chemistry of their resultant behaviors are limitless. Many seniors talk about slacking off, deciding that a particular class is less important than they had imagined. Some hint about not wanting to work so hard and, if the difficult but nonessential class has been avoided until the last year, letting it slide away. Many times they can get away with the "let it slide" attitude; but getting caught in an uneducated plan can be costly, in both time and money.

One high school senior had a rude awakening with the realization that many colleges actually do require three years of a foreign language. The lesson: if you do not have those three years covered in high school, you take them in college. The reality hit home for this family when the tuition bill arrived with a pricey Spanish I class instead of a more pertinent microeconomics course.

Even more disconcerting to parents is the senior's attitude toward the classes taken. One parent winced when her daughter dropped out of a fourth year of German, saying she would wait to see how it was in college. She was anticipating the future but not the future her parents were anticipating. Did she think it would be easier in college? Clearly she didn't want to do the rigorous work rumored to be a part of that advanced high school course. It was only the beginning of a year of backing off, refocusing, and managing parental expectations.

The wind appears to blow freedom the seniors' way. The senior is eager to practice such lines as "I don't have to do that, I'm a senior." These words have full resonance only when uttered by a senior who is in a mood to be instructive and who has waited a long time for the privilege of differentiating himself. It seems they are sharpening their skills for what lies ahead, and the new breeze teases them into a denial of the need for studying regardless of the difficulty of their classes, of the need even to attend class, and certainly of the need to have real explanations of places, times, and curfews. Suddenly, an urgency appears about avoiding the responsibilities and confines of the school structure, actually, any structure, especially that previously employed and enjoyed by parents.

Eric exercised his power after receiving early acceptance to the school of his choice. He had worked hard for three years and it had paid off with this early acceptance, but, sliding into a senior somnolence, he did nothing for the next five months. He didn't do another thing until his English teacher called him into her office to say that he would not be graduating unless he spent the last two weeks of school completing every assignment he had missed since December. The F went to a B in those two weeks, proving, probably, that anything is actually possible with truly focused attention.

Everything is truly relative, we see it all the time. In a visit to the high school yearbook office, friends and I were captivated by the attitude of the seniors toward us; they were our peers. The embarrassment they would have felt to be with a group of adults in their space as freshmen had left them; the silliness of sophomores was nowhere to be found; the "invisible-to-us attitude" of juniors was gone; and they were genuinely interested in what we were doing and how they could help. We did not misunderstand that their attitude prevailed, in part, because no one was related to us.

There's a lot going on for them as well as for us, as parents. They are busy anticipating the glory of the future and we're in a balancing act: trying to hold onto the treasures of the past while attempting to open a door in our hearts to embrace it all. Meanwhile, that very same ritual of beginnings stirs a more complicated elixir in the student.

Mixed feelings are common, both for parents and for their children. We are giving up a place in our lives as they are giving up a place in theirs. One woman wrote, "Right now our son as a senior is really feeling his independence and is off at a moment's notice with his friends. We don't see him a lot. I know it's nature's way of preparing us for separation, but I don't like it. I think back to those days when he was cuddly, warm, submissive, obedient–and I realize I enjoyed that control. He's a special young man whom we'll really miss, but at the same time we're very excited for him and the many adventures awaiting him."

Mother Nature comforts us by having things happen gradually, especially the slipping away of places we've loved. Year by year we come to know less about our children's lives, finding ourselves more on the outside of conversations, hearing fewer details, asking less intrusive questions, and being toughened up ever so slowly.

The toughening process really begins with the end of our carpooling years. Every parent knows that most of the information about one's children comes through those quick jaunts to school, practice, or lessons! Things changed when they got phones in their rooms, almost completely cutting us off from any information obtained from overhearing half of a conversation.

When they went on to get their driver's licenses, as easy as it made our lives, we knew in our hearts that it meant exponentially more autonomy for them and that we'd have very little information from then on. Gradually, parents are relegated to the region of the less informed as the kids in their unerring process move themselves toward more independence. The time line is curious because what seems to take a long time to the kids seems to be only a blink of a parent's watchful eye.

As though we are searching for fireflies at dusk, these hints are barely perceptible, and yet we know. The familiar twitter of a fresh school year awakens parents and we stave off recognition of the finality of this chapter. The excitement overshadows so much of the dread that we should really follow the lead of the seniors and lighten our own schedules, socialize, and enjoy our time together. This is one great thing that kids do, perhaps better than anyone else, and it's just a savvy strategy to follow suit.

The senior year seems to have a life of its own driven by tradition, a structure students cleave to and cherish. Even if they aren't involved in school activities, and half of the seniors don't go to their proms and a third don't attend graduation ceremonies, it is still hard to avoid the power of the ritual. Indeed, they have watched the progressions of those before them, pacing through the scheduled rituals: the festivities of the football season, the dances sprinkled like confetti throughout the year, homecoming elevated to a coronation in which they finally know the names of the people in the court, the winter ball, the all-important senior prom, the yearbook to remind them of what it was, and finally graduation itself as ritual closure.

As we try to lighten their load, save them pain, or spare them hurt, we see the same attitude of denial and independence that we ourselves displayed in a far distant time. Having been there ourselves, we can recognize it in our kids as part of the process of becoming sturdy enough to rise up on those two feet, define that new persona, and move into those adult selves. The disquieting thing is that the separation process has more bumps and bruises than we probably expected, since we are novices on the other side of the process. Surely this proving ground is one aspect of the famous School of Hard Knocks.

The surge of senior power is palpable. One favorite avenue for its expression is the premier position in the car, the so-called "shot-gun" front rider's seat. Underclassmen and younger siblings can only sigh in acceptance. We watch, with private suppressed hilarity, the exaggerated style of the senior moving toward the automobile: It tells all!

Nothing of body language is quite so expressive and precise as the senior "swagger," even from the passive or introverted, and it is always ready to be exercised. If some unwitting, younger, less self-inflated adolescent suffers a memory lapse and has the temerity to look as if he might have thought about taking that seat, he will be promptly rebuked. Nothing in the world bespeaks incredulity in the manner of a senior laying claim to something considered his territory by right of chronological position. It takes your breath away, but it's just part of the senior landscape. It actually helps us know who all the seniors are!

There are a variety of media where the seniors see themselves and leave their mark. One is the yearbook itself which is the most permanent and revered. Some others are the last will and testament, the senior slide show and the class prophecy. The yearbooks are viewed ardently, students hoping they'll be mentioned in the class prophecy, excited about their formal pictures and any small mention. One boy sat quietly wondering: Best personality? Most likely to succeed? Instead, most likely to be late for his own wedding!

A sure sign of that special senior self-awareness which breaks out early upon the taking of the senior pictures. Many of these prize photos–the ones that will linger through lifetimes as the "senior" persona encapsulated–are scheduled the summer before, making the kids feel for the first time that they truly are seniors. Whether the setting is formal or informal, it may very well be the first show of senior self-expression, with a tangible legacy: that revealing senior visage hopefully gazing outward, ahead, alone.

Senior self-assertion or not, parents still may have some important influence. Witness one football mother whose son's team had scheduled a head-shaving session (Yes!) for a Friday afternoon. Her son had not yet had his senior picture taken when he announced to his mother that he was going to participate in this team activity. The farsighted mother, scrambling quickly into action, lined up a photographer and accompanied the son at 1:00 P.M. Friday for the picture taking. The son went from the photo studio directly to the shaving party. That particular parental scheduling and chauffeuring may have been among the last of those duties for that mom, but she realized the importance and the impact those senior pictures would have later in the year when they would appear for all eternity in the yearbook, a lasting memento for friends and family. A lasting gesture of goodwill. The boy's college counselor, however, commented that his children would probably look through his yearbook and say, "Dad, wouldn't it have been cool if you had shaved your head like the guy next to you?"

One senior girl in a very strict parochial school tells of racing from her senior-picture appointment in the gym straight to the restroom to remove her makeup before any nun could see her. Wearing makeup in that school earned demerits and one too many of those could deny graduation. It was a big risk, but that senior power asserted itself: The self-image in the senior pictures was that important.

Looking at the whole senior picture scene, one mother summed it up saying, "They invented themselves in front of the camera . . . and then stared and stared at their created product."

But, the product is changing moment to moment, and there are times when it's hard to keep the tentatively balanced family equanimity. The emerging ego with its newly defined, unpolished edges can grate against parents and test the status quo with raw, abrasive assertion, struggling for new ground in the effort to evolve.

A mother of back-to-back seniors remarked that her daughter was accelerating the pace set by her brother who had left for college the previous year. There were more of those bordering-on-disgust pauses with her daughter demanding a rationale for boundaries. The daughter's explanation that she was almost gone from the household seemed to wrap it up for the daughter, crystallized in her statement: "Don't you trust me? Next year I'll be on my own, what are you going to do then?" It didn't wash with the mother and remained unsettling for both.

Similarly, another example arose following the Broncos Super Bowl XXXII victory. A celebration started in downtown Denver. When a high school senior announced she was going with her friends, her parents tried to dissuade her, giving lengthy recaps of the recent Denver Avalanche team's Stanley Cup celebration party-turned-riot. Defiantly, the girl said: "How can you be like this? I'm an adult!" Receiving reluctant permission given under duress, she went. She was horrified at the behavior she witnessed and luckily left just before the tear gas was sprayed. Was it a lesson learned? Hopefully, but probably not. If the Broncos were to win again tomorrow, she'd want to go again.

One family of a teenager who struggled against them for acceptance and self-esteem said resignedly of their feelings simply that she was, "Seventeen." That was as definitive an explanation as they had for watching her be exclusively with her friends, ignore the parents as much as possible, and proceed very independently with her life. It didn't feel very good to the parents. They had done everything they knew to help and guide her but the relationship still felt lonely and disappointing to them.

The "seventeen" diagnosis could be applied to a variety of behaviors that are foreign and mostly unwelcome to parents. The repertoire seems to burst forth almost unwittingly in surly, snappish, even silly comments. Perplexed, parents can wonder if they are acquainted with the person standing before them. If the comments stand alone, they are often abrupt and offensive, occasionally supercilious, smarmy, and sassy. Now and then, one might be downright rude, ridiculous, rowdy, or even angry. If their comments are viewed as an expression of the turbulent and tempestuous inner being before us who may not have the skills or the sense to moderate or to contemplate the situation, it will be easier to watch.

It's our seniors' psychological chore to break away from us so they will be able to forge an identity all their own. In the deep unconscious there lurks a fright that they might not get it done. Our kids must guard against that and complete their assigned "chore" even if it can't be consciously expressed. The quiet, unnamed fear is more often the culprit in these abrasive encounters, but every young person has an episode or two of this, especially in stressful times.

It may be difficult to pinpoint the precise overt cause of any such eruption, since the seismic source is hard to trace. It may be so ephemeral as to be untraceable. The litany of possibilities, however, may include:

- Not making the team
- Making the team
- Not having a prom date
- Having a boyfriend/girlfriend
- Not having a boyfriend/girlfriend
- Receiving a less-than-desired grade
- Not passing the class
- Not dressing correctly
- Being dressed correctly but still feeling awful
- Not getting braces
- Getting braces
- Because it is before noon
- Not belonging
- Belonging but not in "the" group
- Not getting into a college
- Not being able to afford college
- Because it is nearly December
- Because friends have become weird

- Not having a car
- Having an imperfect complexion
- Being fat
- Being thin
- Being shy
- Because the weather is rainy
- Parents' behavior which now embarrasses them
- Siblings' behavior which always embarrasses them
- Because it is the afternoon
- Because it is Tuesday

It isn't always full-blown arrogance being expressed, either. What passes for indifference on the outside may be reflective of the power surge, but the ambivalence just below the surface tells another, equally powerful story. The leap from this incredibly heady, powerful senior year to the uncharted territory of what's next on the new frontier hits with the power of a left hook the instant the students realize they are moving on.

Late in January, we watched a senior who was a panelist at a pre-orientation meeting for parents of the incoming freshman class. She was the last of six panelists and was hoping to talk about something a little different. She was known for her speaking abilities before an audience and for her enthusiasm for the high school's attributes. Her presentation began in her predictably perky, animated fashion.

She started to talk about how much she personally had benefited from the school and how much she loved the students and the teachers, then she moved along, gracefully saying, "I am going to miss it so when I leave." It seemed as if at the precise moment she uttered those words, it hit her for the first time that she was leaving. She stopped talking, covered her mouth, began sobbing quietly, struggled to regain her composure, finally gave up, and handed the microphone to the moderator.

Everyone we spoke with told of the way Mother Nature prepared us for their children's departure by having them gone most of the time during their senior year. The time to talk is so limited that we may overlook the opportunity to listen carefully if it is presented. There are times when it can be of enormous benefit to watch and gain from an intermediary visiting with our kids, a superb time to be silent ourselves and learn a great deal for our restraint. A perfect lesson in listening!

A case in point for us presented itself one evening when my husband, my son, an old friend, and I were seated in a Chicago restaurant. My friend began talking to my son, then a senior in high school, and because she hadn't seen him in quite awhile, went straight to the heart of the matter:

QUESTION ONE: "Do you still have a girlfriend?"

ANSWER: "No." (News to us, we thought the homecoming date was still a girlfriend.)

QUESTION TWO: "What are you thinking about college?"

ANSWER: "Right now I just know I don't want to stay in-state." (This was more information than we had been able to extract in months.)

QUESTION THREE: "Are there any schools that appeal to you right now?"

ANSWER: "I am thinking seriously of Cornell." (What if he saw us, realized we were there and stopped talking? I wished for the power mentally to send a few more questions to my friend so we could finish this productive visit.)

But, the waiter approached and the conversation ended.

Something subtly informs seniors that the status quo is only a moment in time. They know they have been in the freshman place of no power and they will return there after this temporary joy ride through influence and position. Seniors are on top and ready to be free, yet underneath simmers the anxiety about that first step to freedom and the comfort left behind. It is indeed good to feel on top, as most seniors do. Yet saying good-bye to something this special brings with it the inevitable combination of sadness over the departure and the sharp-edged fear of the unknown.

Being King of the Hill has its advantages and its perils. It is at once protection for the King and the courtiers, providing the opportunity for culturally sanctioned authority and status. This new persona hides vulnerability and the uncertain sense that what is passing will not come again, but makes it possible for the King to play out the role prescribed. Layer by layer then, the newly emerging person comes into being and everything is changed forever. Long live the King!

One Potato,
Two Potato,
Three Potato,
Four

One of the most potent revelations for seniors during this eventful year is that everyone–best friends, pals, classmates–will be making life-defining choices for themselves from now on and the decisions will have little to do with what has happened earlier between friends. The new choices will have to mirror the expectancy and self-definition of every senior and how they hope to see their lives proceed. The choices themselves are an assertion that there is sufficient personal identity to move forward, beyond the present, and even best friends must concede that they may have to pursue different roads. The power of this process is stunning and may be even stupefying to many kids. Not because they really didn't see it coming, but because it just surprises them when the moment is at hand. Earlier, it had seemed as if there were so much time.

The college-application process is a major stage for new decision making. Though there is a separate route for each, there are parallel markers in the journey: the research, perhaps the college trip, the application procedure, and its resolution. The prescribed pieces of the senior year form a context for the constant, gentle reminders of the richness of tradition, provided month by month through the school year. The rising tide lifting all boats the same.

The power and excitement of the exalted senior year provide contrast and backdrop to the humbling and tedious college-application process. The strange and surprising thing is that if this turns into an untouchable topic at the dinner table, or if you've prayed for a crystal ball, you're safely within the normal statistical range of the bell curve bulge—not that it may be particularly comforting to know that, but it's true. Perhaps the escapist mentality that mesmerizes us at times is our own internal preparation and we hope that eventually all of this is going to be all right. We just have to outlast the siege!

During the application mayhem it's probably safe to assume that life outside of the home is sailing along just fine, but home is where the ambivalence rears its trying head. As wearisome as ambivalence is for families at times, it shows that the struggle for self-definition still draws from the powerful place of origin, seeking assurance, encouragement, and validation—even if it doesn't sound like that very often. Life feels more like a territorial, only semirational exercise in which we parents make little difference. Our electronic equipment, at least, is saved by surge protectors which spare it from outrageous power eruptions in its system. We parents—even the best of us—have only our good intentions and best intuition; for each of us, it's an uncharted course with many variables.

One weary mom called the application process second only to toilet training in disagreeable parenting responsibilities. Since she had assumed the toilet-training task years before, she felt a sense of delayed fairness in giving the college-application job to her husband. It would have helped had he been alerted to adolescent mood swings so as not to have taken them so personally, but everyone survived the episode and everyone learned something—even if it was not what they had in mind at the beginning.

The unassailable incongruity the senior feels was evident at a junior-high basketball game one December night. The valedictorian of the local high school was in the stands watching her twelve-year-old brother shoot hoops. This bright young woman was casually jotting down some thoughts. When asked what homework she was completing, she smiled and said, "I'm just writing my essay for the Georgetown {University} application." Through a grim smile, her mother added that it had to be postmarked the following day. Was the daughter stalling, did she really think she had this under control, or was this court-side activity a hint of ambivalence?

One bemused mother tells the story of her daughter who had completed three applications when the fourth arrived from the University of Notre Dame. The girl carefully read through the application and announced that she had decided not to apply there. Knowing that she couldn't ask too much, the mother gently inquired, "Why not?" The daughter said very seriously, "Of the three essays I've already written, nothing fits their question. So, I won't be applying there." And she didn't.

Jack had been a good student until his appointment with his high school counselor early in his senior year. A young man with good grades and a very high ACT (American College Test) score, he had wanted to go to the University of Michigan. The counselor discouraged him from his dream and suggested lowering his sights, which sadly seemed to be the beginning of his decline. At graduation he had applied to two other state schools but couldn't make a decision. His parents left deposits at both schools because he was paralyzed with indecision and depression. As much as we think our kids aren't listening to us, I think they hear more than we believe.

Our hopes that something will make it easier to let go can get pinned to small wishes—early college acceptance, for example. Indeed, while many are avoiding sending in those all-important applications, others have applied to be accepted early. This, too, is a mixed bag. It does take care of the anxiety of waiting, but it makes room for a different kind of anxiety. When a student applies for and declares the intention to seek early acceptance, it is a declaration of intent to attend if accepted. With that decision to seek early acceptance come the questions Did I make the right decision? and What if I change my mind? Some schools penalize heavily for this error.

Other students take early acceptance as the symbolic end of academic studies and find it nearly impossible to care about grades despite knowing a final transcript will go out to their college. Parents talk about feeling relief that the search is over on one hand, but then, in the same breath talk about how it shortened the already-too-brief experience of being a part of the journey, even if it was just writing checks.

An important pitfall to avoid at this time is the trap many of the kids bait just hoping to get the parents to make the decision for them or at least to declare their colors. Many times the conversations go like this:

> STUDENT: You want me to go to the University of Parent Alma Mater.
>
> PARENT: I want you to go wherever you will be happy.
>
> STUDENT: But, if you had your way I would go to U of PAM.
>
> PARENT: You will be there four years, you must make the decision.
>
> STUDENT: But, you would have me go to U of PAM if you had your way.
>
> PARENT: I think you would do very well there, but I'm not going to tell you where to go.

This scenario is almost litany. Don't take the bait!

In fact, applying and choosing a college is such a traumatic and specialized arena that a whole industry of college consultants is in place to guide people through these straits. It's an interesting equation: The college consultant knows what parents wish they knew. It can be very beneficial when most parents are overwhelmed with the new routine and the competitiveness that shows its face at every door. The quest begins in the junior year with advice about preparing for the Scholastic Aptitude Test (SAT)—what to take in the senior year, when to take the SAT, and which colleges match the applicant's profile. Consultants can offer help in the matching process, assist in filling out applications and translate what is being requested, and also pursue financial aid. If parents can recognize this as an area of an informational void, college consultants can be truly a godsend.

It's one more lesson in humility, too, as consultants can expose parents' insecurities at every turn. Once we know that the student is telling them what we desperately want to know, the race is on. They hear what students are feeling, what they're desiring or fearing, where they'd like to go to school, what they're ambivalent about, even how they feel about their parents. Parents, knowing on some deep level of the psyche that someone else knows all this, sometimes want to assert their control. Occasionally, this happens in unfortunate ways, such as parents making sure that the student chooses the parents' choice of a college. Or, by demanding that they apply (and get accepted) to a college that is a more gentle intellectual "reach," as they're called. One consultant, recognizing the difficulty of this time for families, says it is the rare case in which a consulting job gets completed without at least one parent becoming ignited by the process.

One mother phoned her college consultant when enraged that the son's SAT scores had arrived with the verbal portion seventy-five points below the other six SATs already taken. The consultant had advised against taking an SAT preparatory course, which now the mother challenged in the most strident manner. The consultant sighed, knowing there was nothing she could say at that point. The mother went on to say that her son knew all the words included in the verbal portion because she had quizzed him on them for months. Not only had the mother opened her son's mail, she had projected her own expectations, fears and hopes onto her son, thus diminishing his senior-year experience by requiring such an overwhelming amount of study time, preparation time, and exhausting days of taking seven tests.

It is almost guaranteed that the more times one takes the SAT, the harder it is to concentrate on the test. The advice given by the majority of high-school counselors is to have kids take the test once at the end of their junior year and once at the beginning of their senior year. The usual experience is that the scores vary seventy-five points one way or the other, but it is rare to find more difference than that.

A veteran college consultant, with more than twenty-five years in the field, reports still being awed by the college-application process as it transpires today. She describes a world of big business, watching the focus shifting from the most important part of the process, the student, to an ugliness that might find its match only in archetypal overly competitive Little League baseball parent behavior. She sees college application as a brand name business involving more competitive parents to make more of the decisions than the kids themselves, with the kids being the ones to lose in the end.

Only a certain number of students will attend those sought-after brand name schools. The others need to find a place, too, and luckily there are many schools which work well. For success, the student's comfort needs to be the foremost concern, college consultants say. They must find a place where they can live and learn. The comforts focused on include size of school, climate, activities, the typical student, the nearby community, availability of other activities, proximity to home, and other individual priorities. A student's background often dictates comfort, especially as it relates to urban/rural preference, religious priorities, and ethnic diversity. A first assessment probably is asking the seniors to make a list of factors that would make them feel comfortable, and that may be a parental eye-opener!

Rhea, a seasoned consultant with words of wisdom, offered her wish that we begin to realize how we are robbing our kids of their senior year when they are pushed too hard or influenced toward places they don't want to see. Any parent of a senior knows that gentle prodding is all part of the process, but causing undue anxiety isn't helpful at this vulnerable time. Listen carefully to the kids; they are speaking infrequently and softly, but authentically.

The process, taking place alongside the regular class activities and responsibilities, adds a dimension of stress and distress to a busy year, even though simultaneously it can be filled with hope and expectancy. It's actually quite bold for an adolescent to assert himself in an adult academic world, announcing that he is worthy (well, probably) to join you, and certainly hoping for acceptance. (Do parents forget the pit-of-the-stomach experience this once was, or is it easy to put that memory aside?) The risk taking is enormous for someone seventeen or eighteen. It takes all the bravado and bravery imaginable. And, once all the applications are in, the initial responses have been received, you've talked with the counselors, and every last test has been taken, along comes another momentous leap–the college tours.

Follow the
Yellow Brick Road

Between the cockiness of the senior year and the innocence of the new horizons come the much anticipated yet feared college tours. After the analytical research of the type, location, academic strengths, library capacities, reputed social life indicators, and financial factors have been compared among desirable colleges, the search must narrow to the most probable. In order to get the real flavor of things, many families take their senior on one or more trips to view personally the campuses being considered. Many others huddle around the kitchen table over the various brochures. However this process moves ahead, the moment of decision closes in.

A friend who's been with an airline for thirty years says that kids and their parents who are on college trips can be spotted a mile away. "They're the ones who aren't talking to one another. There is a frown on the face of the student and a blank look on the face of the parent," she said, adding, "they never look at one another and they hold books and magazines for hours without turning a page." Poor parents! Poor kids! The tumult of the story as it transpires is so overwhelming that it's hard to be a player. It's hard to know the script and it's hard to follow the part they've been given.

Being recruited for a sport (or anything!) helps. One student athlete was sought by the coach at one of his favorite colleges and his parents booked flights immediately. The boy was given the Red Carpet Tour. He saw every inch of the campus, visited with students, and was complimented by the team members who wanted him to accept the offer to play with them the following season. He was encouraged by the admissions office and given a nice financial package. As he prepared to leave, the coach and admissions director asked if he had any questions after seeing everything. His mother cringed when he said with worldly aplomb, "Yes, do you have a linen service?" Where did that come from? This response is the perfect example of the tangle of information, emotions, and confusion going through the minds of seventeen- and eighteen-year-old kids who have such a big decision to make.

Parents try to be encouraging and supportive, but just when we think we've caught the excitement of the college adventure, rather than riding the tidal wave of emotion, a simple question sends us reeling. Returning from an emotional fact-finding college trip, one mother said this: "Since our trip, I have recommended to other parents that it not be made with siblings. It was such a bonding time. I can remember sitting on the airplane as we flew from the East Coast to the Midwest. My daughter put her head on my shoulder and fell asleep. I put my arm around her shoulders and as I watched her sleeping, the tears trickled down my cheeks. The man sitting on my left looked over and as he reached up to turn off the light, asked quietly, 'College trip?' I nodded yes and was so touched at his perceptiveness. The feeling that my daughter and I were sharing, that we couldn't get enough of each other as her last spring at home approached, seemed to me then and now to be one that other parents could identify with."

I wanted to show my own son the West Coast schools because my family lived nearby and it would be an efficient solution for me. Besides, I loved the colleges and they were places I wish I had been able to attend. The first college we visited was rejected by him because the buildings didn't match and were too far apart. Since I didn't favor this college, I found that explanation quite reasonable.

However, when we visited my preference, acceptance mattered more to me. I was taken by the wisteria hanging over the old arches, the history of the school and of the area, and the proximity to my own alma mater. Generally I was swept away by the possibilities. School was not in session. The dorms were dark, the bookstore empty, and the campus quiet; when we looked into the cavernous dining area, all we saw were silent fast food outlets—Burger King, Taco Bell, Pizza Hut—no bustling dining hall. I could tell it wasn't clicking with him and carefully asked how he felt. Answer: "I'm sure I'd never get enough to eat there." That took care of the West Coast.

One painful introduction to our exclusion from the process is the secrecy of it all. Question: "What is your first choice in colleges?" Answer: "I don't know." I know we believe that they do know and that they just don't want to tell. It isn't this simple.

When we received this communication from our college-bound son, it was difficult to hear. It was better, though, when safer adults asked him about his first choice. When he told them he genuinely didn't know, I accepted it. It isn't that they don't know. It is that knowing signifies too much. If they say it out loud before they are accepted, then they've just dealt themselves another layer of feelings to cope with should they be rejected. It forces them to be in the future when they're enjoying the present. It is easier to stall.

Be prepared: Kids hate questions. When anyone is asked a question, we know that the inquirer has a reason for asking. A question gives our child something to stonewall. It doesn't work. Cut your losses and begin to make statements instead. "We've got to get moving. These are the deadlines. I'll write the check and you'll need to send it in."

It is even okay to be silly. Give them a list as you did when they were six. "We're going to dinner. Please check the box which indicates your interest: 'yes' or 'no.' " Or even lie on the floor and throw a mock whining tantrum, telling them you can't do it all. In these times when nothing is certain and everything is overwhelming, do anything that works.

In response to an information request, Keith told of receiving letters beginning in his sophomore year from the school he considered his first choice. After two and a half years and countless letters from the school Keith was denied admission. He had mistaken the volume of form letters for a legitimate interest on the part of the college. Similarly, a popular college consultant cautions all athletes she works with to remember that they can be flown all around the country and complimented left and right, but until they have a letter of acceptance in their hands, nothing is certain. Twice she had worked with very gifted student athletes. They were nationally ranked in their sports, had high SAT scores and great grade point averages. They seemed to have what every college would have wanted. Both times they were "recruited"–flown to colleges and given high praise–and had many colleges from which to select. However, both put all their eggs in the proverbial single basket only to be rejected in the end.

Pat watched his son open the first acceptance letter from the local college. "He was guaranteed admission because of his scores and grades but there was still a visible sense of relief that someone wanted him, would accept him if all else fails. Every letter is important even if you don't really want to go there.

"The thrill of the chase is over when that acceptance letter is returned. Just as with school selection, once the choice was made silence enveloped again. He refused to talk about it, refused to express any joy in the selection, didn't talk about fears, was inexcusably, inexplicably, unexpectedly unable to attend a local gathering of first year students/freshmen-to-be from the local area who were going to his new school. We began to wonder whether he regretted his choice and might not go, might go to the local college and give up on all the school criteria that were important and which led to his developing the college list in the first place."

The elusive bird in the hand, the symbolic end of the quest, is metaphoric for this part of the passage. We have all anticipated this time for our kids. We have hoped fervently that they find their dreams and delight in the new opportunities that are coming to them and in which we will not be as directly involved. It's an important milestone to recognize that this time of decisions about the future represents one incremental element of the letting go, for kids as well as parents.

Kids may not cling to the nest as they see a more distant goal. Parents must begin to let them go a little more. Parents do this best if they can muster the maturity and dignity to acknowledge to themselves that the mounting pressures are real, earnest, and necessary. This, actually, is the way things should transpire at this time, gradually. There are more pieces to come, but if at each unfolding stage, parents can acknowledge this natural process and gather all their resources to respond graciously and generously in the letting go, it will be a gift that resonates forever, for them and for their child.

College acceptance can be elusive and there is no easy word for rejection. The sting feels the same for all the euphemisms, and they all hurt. The anguish is often acute for the kids, it sometimes being their first major rebuff and when they're vulnerable following the process of extending themselves and taking the risk. All these kids have put themselves out on a limb. They've taken risks in selecting particular schools, and the payoff is only in an acceptance. Not easy.

Parents share the rejection as well but from the point of remembering their own processes and grieving for their child's tender psyche in this place. It doesn't always help immediately to take a more philosophical view that something better will doubtless come along, but in a strange and somehow miraculous way, it often does. Perhaps it's more that accommodating a new expectation gives the impetus to make it work out regardless. Yet there is much to do in adjusting to a new "given" and making the most of a second choice. It can happen, but it has to follow letting go of the first dream to make room for something different. Neither quick nor easy.

One college consultant provided an interesting but disturbing insight into many colleges' acceptance/rejection process. As schools strive for diversity, students are pressured to differentiate themselves, to become the right type of tile to fit into the mosaic. If they are an identical piece—and many talented students look similar on paper—their spot in the picture may already be filled. If that's the case, they have to look around for other possibilities. A well-rounded, hard-working, bright student is many times in the majority.

"The college takes its shopping cart, runs up and down the aisles, and takes what it wants," says Sarah Myers McGinty, author of *The College Application Essay.*"

"Apparently true, says educational consultant Rusty Haynes in an article for *Rolling Stone Magazine.* He notes, "This year {1996} more than 15,000 students applied to Brown, hoping to be among a freshman class of about 1,400. At Harvard the odds were no less staggering: some 18,000 kids for a class of 1,620 including 2,905 high school valedictorians. One hundred sixty-five of those rejected applicants had scored a perfect 1,600 on the SAT. Both schools along with Princeton, Columbia, Penn, UVA [University of Virginia], and Georgetown, received more applications this year than ever."

Admissions offices at these public universities list discouraging numbers for applicants in 1997. The University of North Carolina received roughly 15,800 applications for a class of 3,200; the University of Colorado, 14,500 for 4,000 places; and the University of Virginia, 16,000 for 5,000 slots. This is the most random piece of unpredictability for the senior.

The dynamics of the college-application process have changed and other factors, such as creativity, perseverance, and leadership can be weighted for indicators of success in college. There are no promises going in and not many sure predictions.

College application is assuredly one of the most difficult passages for students. With such a long, involved process and the inability to control the outcome, we all feel a little vulnerable. Many consultants talk about so-called "safe schools" to which seniors should apply just to provide a backup. There are few safe schools because students are applying to far more than necessary just to get in somewhere, thereby clogging the pipeline and the probabilities. Safe becomes a new relative term.

Counselors encourage students to eliminate the idea of a "first choice." Even this language of not having verbal priorities is helpful because if acceptance comes from an array of good choices, it is just as prized. The opposite, being emotionally committed to a "must-get" school is risky since the choice process is a serendipitous art and not a calculated or predictable science. Taking a safe, flexible position keeps an opening on the middle road, the one without the harshest bumps.

Drew received a full scholarship to a prestigious academic school to play lacrosse. He was thrilled to accept it. He knew he would be one of the starting players as a freshman. His focus was on the sport instead of the school. Counselors will caution students first to choose the most desirable school of the available options to attend, to be sure to love the school, then to think about the sport. Drew couldn't cut it academically at this challenging college and left after just one semester. He had forced a fit and missed many other opportunities as a result.

When a friend of mine told me her daughter had decided against Brown in favor of a state school, my mind was racing. The girl would have been the third generation to attend Brown and it was such an honor to be accepted. Why had she made such a decision? As it turned out, the parents couldn't afford to send her there. When applying to schools, set the parameters. Let the kids know what part of the responsibility will be their portion. Anyone can understand the numbers when we talk about a college education approaching the six-figure range. There are just so many scholarships available. There are just so many loans that people want to take. It's not unusual for people to have to say no to a dream school due to a financial situation. The process must be reality based as well.

One young man knew that the school of his dreams was a financial stretch for his family. On his eighteenth birthday he started buying lottery tickets in hopes of winning the jackpot. No, he didn't win the lottery, but he did have a great bonanza: a $10,000 grant from his chosen school for his track record of hard work.

Maybe there's an element of good luck in many selections, even if they're very different from what might be expected for a student. As we've talked with independent college consultants, they said that given one year, most kids have selected the right school. Somehow even those who appear the least interested in the college search seem to find the one thing that makes a school right for them.

In trying to look ahead to the next experience, parents can unknowingly attempt to work out their own values through providing kids' college educations. Some who worked their way through college feel that it was good for them and made them appreciate the experience, knowing that if they failed to make it through college that at least they were always aware of the options. Others who worked during college talk of having missed out on the freedom of what they saw in their peers and in no way want their kids to work during those years. Still others who were provided for sometimes feel a pressure to provide similarly for their children, yet those who were provided for sometimes feel they missed something by not being involved in the financial obligation themselves. There are many opportunities to disagree.

Add to that the couples whose experiences were extremely different—one who found high school to be a struggle and never attended college, one who was capable but couldn't afford it, one who chose to take care of a family, or those who started and for whatever reason were unable to connect and dropped out. If those feelings are haunting ones, they tend to present themselves in camouflage when making decisions about the children's college experience and can drift into the kid's college years, still stalking, still unresolved. It is common to hear parents talking about how things were different. Along with the discussions about computers, telephones, and freedom is the conversation about what it was like for us in terms of freedom or opportunity. We can't figure out whether to correct what we got by giving it to our children or by not giving it to our children. No one knows what is the "right" solution. In some ways we always feel inadequate regardless of what we do.

Life is filled with choices and making a decision is one of the skills we rely upon throughout adulthood. Few decisions made before a college selection have such lingering and important implications, but once made, the chosen path cuts off other options. It makes a difference to know how to weigh the options and whether one choice or another is of paramount importance, lesser importance, or hardly a blip on the screen. Helping our children see the distinctions at a time when choices are really important and working with them to see and analyze the possibilities are gifts for a lifetime.

If there were only a few large cookie cutters shaping us all into similar beings, it would be an immensely boring world. The wondrous thing about the diversification of personas is that we have wonderful characters in our midst, the ones who are set apart by their own rhythms, their own original expressions that must find a voice, their divergent dreams and purposes. We need to celebrate these extraordinary ones and we need to honor their journey in life. They, after all, have found the courage to be true to their novel, unique, and unrepeatable selves. They do march to different drummers, and the distant tattoo can be heard only by them.

It's not the smoothest course, however, when unique problems do arise. It's a trial for the child because our society values the middle of the stream more than the tributaries and it promises difficulties for the parents of such children as well. One mom, having watched the nontraditional behaviors and choices of her senior son, in a moment of weariness said to him, "It's hard to be a parent of an unconventional kid." She put into words what many parents probably hold inside. To the degree that people have expectations for the "typical" family life, it is hard or harder for everyone.

A family of my long acquaintance had such an experience, which had its tender and endearing moments and its hurdles. The mom, Judy, wrote of her son Sol's experience: "Sol's last year of high school went by so fast, it is a complete blur to me now. We rarely saw him. Between working and his very active social life, it seems as if we only saw him when he was hungry or tired. College was never a major priority in his life. He did manage to fill out a couple of applications and wrote his essays. The day his first acceptance came in, his father and I danced a happy jig. We were so thrilled, and then the second acceptance came—we were so happy for him. Sol, however, never showed much excitement about the whole situation.

"Then, about two months prior to his graduation, Sol was sitting at his desk one night attempting to fill out dormitory applications, when he came downstairs and told us his plans. He told us he just wasn't ready yet to go to college—that there is something else he wanted to do and if he didn't do it then, he worried he never would. We hadn't a clue what this might be. Then he told us he wanted to go to California and become a STUNTMAN, of all things. We told him he was on his own in researching the deal, but we'd support him if that is what he chose to do.

"Anyway, he researched the field, found a school and all. So we went to California and checked out the school, met the instructor, asked a lot of questions, and

Sol was very excited about this whole new adventure. I cried a lot inside." This whole period is not the student's singular experience, it involves the whole family as never before.

Many have stories of the mild and well-meaning passage that is simply different from the norm. Still others, for different reasons, have wildly disparate and difficult times. Many students face tough decisions and experience excruciating disappointments. It is a regular lament to college counselors (and less so one shared with parents) that a bad grade in that overwhelming high school freshman year keeps their grade point average sagging too low for application to their favored college. Others experience family difficulties that consume their energy and their emotional and financial resources. The harshness of teenage peer pressure is still evident as well.

Let's not leave out the dramatic avoidance employed by a few: deliberate flunking. Teachers talk about this with great helplessness and dismay. One high school administrator told of students who knew they weren't graduating yet couldn't find a way to tell their families. Some even tried to acquire caps and gowns to give the impression that they were graduating. Occasionally whole families showed up for graduation, some from out of town, only to find that the student had not met the requirements to graduate. It's hard to imagine that denial could take such a firm hold of someone, but denial is a powerful and entrenched mechanism, one that is hard to put aside or climb out of easily or gracefully.

Sometimes what seems to be unique expression is really a reflection of deep and conflicted passages: trouble in the family relationships as many long-term marriages begin to flounder with the advent of the children leaving home; trouble with the law related to drugs or alcohol; serious problems with girl or boyfriend relationships including pregnancy and abortion, addictions and inappropriate use of drugs or alcohol; aberrations of skin decoration (tattoos or piercings) as a countercultural statement; a heightened incivility reflecting a disconnection with society at large; and even suicide, as some extreme examples. The problems for some kids are enormous, crushing, and defeating. Often they find no one to turn to for help, especially if parents have absented themselves. There are desperate and grievous things that happen today in greater numbers than before, and to the extent that such events affect any among us, they actually affect us all.

So often, high school is a time when lost souls find the pressure to belong so intense as to be irresistible, leading them onto a path of destruction. One mother relayed a story of her son, Ben, who at sixteen years of age, started dating for the first time. The girl was a flirt, a tease, and needed a great deal of attention following her parents' bitter divorce. Ben was crazy about her. When she suggested that he try pot, he did. To impress her? To fit in? To rebel? Whatever the reason, Ben found his way from ultra-conservatism and good grades to the world of substance abuse and depression. He is nineteen years old now and on his way back from the living hell he imposed on himself and his family. He missed much of his senior year, drifted, but finally graduated. He hasn't gone to college and realizes now that he wants that experience. Three years were lost, but he made a brave and constructive course correction. Some of these stories have happy landings.

Problems with drugs are not as atypical as they once were. Drugs are the worst nightmare imaginable. Hard to predict, hard to recognize, and hardest to resolve. Many young people cannot find the connection with their peers, family, or with an inner sense of guidance to advise them. Addictions of many sorts are more prevalent as we become disaffiliated with our basic connections to life, and they are a dangerous and dispiriting attempt to fill the emptiness that young people can feel. One senior girl said blankly, "I just don't know why we're here." There was no connection, no understanding of something more to existence, no saving grace. No amazing grace.

Sadly, some expressions of individuality are negative. But, many, many are positive affirmations of a growing character. Maybe we need more tolerance of and encouragement for all the divergent drummers among us. They are the ones, after all, who have the courage to be their own special selves and who are trying hard to listen to their own voice singing in the chorus. It takes all of us—the chorus, the band, and here or there a kazoo or two—to make music together.

Pomp and Circumstance

Few pieces of music convey to us the full regal sense of ceremony that *Pomp and Circumstance* does. It tells us as much about graduation as the processions of caps and gowns; the high jinx; the pranks, parties, and pratfalls. When we hear the first chords against the backdrop of the massed diplomas, members of the school board, teachers, and the principal we know all the pieces are in place.

Graduation, the grand finale to this amazing year, is a very special rite of passage, one of the few rituals we have maintained with the vigor and attention it deserves. We still name a valedictorian. We still don caps and gowns. We still congratulate and share the splendor with those we love. It becomes the day we remember—everything about it: the ceremony, the weather, the next-door-neighbor child's antics, the romp and the circumspect. In some way, graduation tells us that the graduates have cleared the hurdle, made the grade, passed the test, settled the account. In short, they've made it. We notice by our pageant, and we all can celebrate together!

There's no real way to catalog all the feelings present at one single graduation ceremony. The graduates–their faces bright, excited, animated, and filled with hope–also reflect relief, gratitude upon completion, sadness upon leaving, and an unspoken yearning for what it was or wasn't. Any one graduate has a flood of shifting emotions at the very moment of the ceremony. All of them are doubtless amazed it has caught them this way, so ready to celebrate yet so awash in surging tides of emotions. They might ask themselves, "Who could have anticipated all of this?"

But the graduates' emotional range is matched or actually bested by that of the parents', who, of course, share all the fervor of the graduates themselves, having lived so close to the drama the preceding years. They know exactly what it means on one level, but they add to it the surging feelings of their generation, one which has already experienced their own ceremony in its time. The reminiscence of that earlier pageant added to the heady brew of the parental perspective allows them to know the trials and joys of bringing this person to this point. And, then, wouldn't you know they would play *Pomp and Circumstance?* The parents' eyes are brightly shining, brimming, all over again.

Looking back at the ceremony, most graduates recount a blurred, gauzy version of what actually happened, what the speakers said, how they received their diplomas, and what occurred after that. It all seems to have passed in a moment of partial awareness. It lingers after as an important piece of growing up, important as an acknowledgment of their work and achievement, and important because it is how our culture passes the baton. They remember the school orchestra playing, the microbursts of flashbulbs creating a simulation of fireworks. They remember if they could spot their families in the audience. The high relief of the exquisite details of the ceremony itself seem to drift away. Mostly, in recollection, they just know they were there and they have graduated. The blur is enough.

One college freshman when asked about his graduation ceremony said it was too long and he could think only of wanting out of it. When asked what he felt when it had ended, he said, "Oh, it all ended midway through the second semester."

In fact, some years, the graduation ceremony itself is considered an aside by numbers of students who manage to miss it. For other kids, being there is still very important. On the way to her graduation ceremony, Kelly asked her parents to please stop quickly at the hardware store. Already in her cap and gown, she ran into the store, made her purchase, and hurried back to the car. The family raced to graduation and dropped her at the football stadium. As the parents scanned the hundreds of graduates with their binoculars, into clear view came a cap with a huge red heart on the top. They'd found her! The reason for stopping at the hardware store? Red electrical tape.

Other times it is obvious that our being there is important. A mom with a twinkle in her eye tucked a little disposable camera into her son's pocket so he could take pictures of the graduates up close. As the procession started, the young man turned to his parents and snapped their photo.

Sometimes it is clear that things mean too much to people. Parents were universally disappointed when a rent-a-plane carrying a long message tail of congratulations started circling an outdoor graduation ceremony, drowning out the young man delivering a meaningful speech to his class. To everyone's dismay, the commotion interrupted the entire ceremony. Of course, parents are proud of their graduate, but once in a while, their pride more dramatically demonstrates an incomplete linkage of considerate thought.

Perhaps the best we can hope for is that we're prepared. When the graduates are asked to stand up and turn their tassels, we are aware that this ritual, repeated over the years, signals the true end of high school. They are on their way.

The fun at graduation does not end with the ceremony. The graduation parties that begin the week before graduation seem to continue throughout the entire summer. One party asked the graduates to come dressed as they saw themselves in ten years. Another was a luncheon following the ceremony given by 30 families at a large club where all of the family members and 120 friends gathered. The senior-class parents of one large high school in Denver invited the entire class to the Union Depot, a cavernous facility big enough to hold everyone, so no one was left out. My favorite invitation read, "Free at Last." The modes of the celebrants are varied and personal, but the happy theme is all the same!

Rebekah said she didn't want a big-deal party, she just wanted something where they could all be together. Her mother asked her to make a list of invitees and her idea of a menu. Two days later the menu was on the kitchen table.

- Cake - half chocolate, half white but the taste doesn't matter; it must simply be ordinary and on the other hand, the looks must be spectacular with bright intense purple and yellow roses and sunflowers
- Fingers - like baklava but easier to eat because of their shape
- Rice Krispy treats - hauled on the plane by Aunt Debbie who is quintessential Rice Krispy material
- Brownies - made by Mom and divine with a crispy outer edge
- Cherry shortbread bars - melt-in-your-mouth to-die-for from sister Sarah
- Strawberry rhubarb crisp already made by Mom and in the freezer
- Blueberry ginger crisp, and on the dessert front an ice cream sundae bar
- A big green salad with sugared almonds, mandarin oranges, and a yummy dressing
- Asparagus marinated in raspberry vinaigrette
- Vegetable tray from Meijer's with ranch dressing and gherkin pickles
- Woody's Mediterranean salad of tomatoes, cucumbers, maybe celery, green peppers
- Woody's humus and pita bread
- Woody's vegetarian grape leaves
- Woody's tabbouleh but Dad wants to make his less-fat version
- Woody's vegetarian kibbe if they can make them in little ball size rather than huge potato size
- Woody's falafel balls with tahini and yogurt sauces
- Chicken wings—as in THE famous ones

- Meatballs with sweet and sour sauce by Mom
- Giant subs–half with turkey, half with ham from Jersey Giant
- A carved watermelon with a handle, filled with fresh fruit.

And, said Mom, she wanted strawberries and pretzels for dipping in chocolate sauce, which Mom suggested was entirely her own responsibility if it was to happen.

One of the most difficult discussions associated with the graduation parties is the stand the parents take on serving alcohol to the kids. One mother asked her son to get the list of guests together and he asked if she were going to permit drinking. When she gave an emphatic "No!", he said he'd rather not have a party. They didn't. There are some parents, however, who will allow alcohol at the parties. We can't close our eyes to this fact. This situation brings up two issues: what you say, if anything, to those parents, and what you say to your senior.

If parents are uncomfortable with this situation, as many of us are, it is appropriate to tell those involved that you don't support serving alcohol to minors. Other than telling your senior, who is quite possibly eighteen, that you are uncomfortable, your options are limited. Having parties with other families seems to make it easier with more parents taking this stand against alcohol. Some invitations will read "no alcohol permitted–must have invitation to attend." One mother sent a credit card with her son to take a cab home if need be. Another insisted her son take her cellular phone to call for a ride home if necessary. Draw your line, set your parameters, and communicate these decisions to your senior.

When one exhausted graduate came home early the evening of back-to-back-to-back graduation parties, he slouched at the table saying, "I thought you said we'd go out to dinner tonight." The parents had planned dinner out but didn't know he would be with them. When asked if he'd accompany them, he said, "Please take me with you–I can't do one more graduation party right now." The graduation pace, regardless of the refreshments served, is overwhelming.

After graduation and during the parties comes a last-time event of significant importance for parents: the last time you will have to hound your child to write thank-you notes! While the graduation gifts pile up as high as the activity list is long, the thank-you note task sinks to the bottom of the priority list. After the last note is however tardily written, the parents can celebrate one step ahead on their own rite of passage–checking off the thank-you note badgering task from their list of unpleasant parenting chores!!

Our lives are busy and so preoccupied that the rituals we have to mark the major transitions are not given the time and the attention that they deserve. We are distracted by so many "things" in our lives that we hurry through even the most important events in life. Perhaps our greatest gift would be to ask of our children (and participate with them) in making and taking the time to enjoy the true miracle of the graduation. In a transforming moment, everyone is now in a different relationship to one another. Newly formed by this passage are the parents' relationships with each other and with the kids and the new graduates with their parents and other siblings. It's so stunning, it's hard to grasp the significance.

"Sunrise, Sunset, Swiftly Flow the Years . . ."

As we realize the depth of our children's uncertainties, it helps us immensely if we are allowed to feel their longing. But, even if we aren't allowed in, many of us vow to be better balanced and not let our conflicting feelings dampen our enthusiasm and participation in our child's emancipation. As much as we want to perform this job well, however, it is easier to declare so than to execute when this last high school year introduces us to the last of everything. At first it is just the parents who realize the finality of the times, starting with that "last first day of school." Then we struggle through the last back-to-school night, parent-teacher conferences, the last football game or swim meet. Our sense of time and timing probably harkens back to our own passage, but we see and feel and sense the strong current pulling us along.

All of this occurs while the students appear to be thinking it isn't the last but simply the "best of everything." What a great attitude! As difficult as the good-byes will be, today is fun, the future is exciting, and they are on top of the world. If we're lucky, they have that strong self-esteem we've tried all their lives to help them develop. This is the power boost that affirms an incredible life just from being on top, just from being a senior and having the best of the known world.

I watched one strong, confident, loving dad squeeze every moment out of his son's final swim meet. The dad shared both the exhilaration of the victory and the poignancy of the finality of the last time in that uniform, of the smell of the chlorine and musty bags, of the team camaraderie, and of the immediacy of it all. It was easier for the parents at the swim team banquet a week later without the sounds, the smells, and the feelings which were then memories rather than the moment.

Jayne wrote that you first realize your child will be leaving when you take a break from the havoc of everyday teenage life and realize that next year they won't be here and think, "Next year at Halloween she'll be in another place, another city, with new friends and a new life. This is when the panic sets in! We raise our children to be intelligent, independent free spirits, who will one day spread their wings and fly.

"When 'one day' approaches, a mom's first instinct is to grab her, hold her close, and not let the big bad world take away your flower. My daughter's pediatrician told me that the first time a daughter goes on a date, you feel like you are handing a Stradivarius to a gorilla. This thought applies to my daughter. I'm sending a Stradivarius to the world. Will she ever play the same music at home? You have worked to prepare your child for this time in her life. Have we worked to prepare the parents for this time?

"Halloween was a 'red letter' awakening for me," she continues. "Every year on October 31, for the last 17 years, we have made Manwiches, Mom's French fries, and hot apple cider and watched the Disney animated version of *The Legend of Sleepy Hollow*. No matter if there were neighborhood kids, friends, family, casts of thousands, or just us, between after school and bedtime, we had our own Halloween ritual.

"This past year Lindsey had plans, no time for Manwiches or fries, no time for cider. Friends were going someplace else for a school activity. She was off, but by 9:00 P.M. she was home. She came in and said, 'Hey Mom, can we watch the movie together?' We did! It was great for me and she knew she was giving me a moment to hold dear."

As we'll realize more and more, holidays mark this rite of passage in special ways. They are striking reminders of years spent together and how things may change. It is not unusual to try to make that final assured holiday gathering perfect. In our own family, I had decided that this "last" Thanksgiving would be the one in which I asked the boys what they'd like to do, hoping they'd recite all of the special traditions I had grown up with and had built into my own family life. These two, who are never in agreement except in opposition to their parents, quickly said: "Anything but turkey." I had been so open about the invitation that I had to ask, "What, then, would you like?" With little delay they said, "Well, how about ham or pizza?"

Defeated, I asked my husband to try to find somewhere for us to be because I didn't want a pizza Thanksgiving in my home. He found us a Residence Inn with a kitchen and proceeded to order the $29.95 special ham dinner for four from a local supermarket. There we were on Thanksgiving day sitting at the card table, eating off plastic plates with paper-thin metal forks, ham the pink that only synthetic can duplicate, watching Chevy Chase in *Christmas Vacation*. At the time I believe I said, "This all seems to fit together." The next morning when we left the motel, both boys climbed into the car and said, "This is the best Thanksgiving we've ever had." Mission accomplished, I suppose.

Conflicting feelings about change are also shown in endearing ways. Kids seem to hang onto tradition, hoping to keep things the same. For the past ten years we have hosted a children's Christmas party, replete with a Father Christmas, small whimsical gifts for each child, and an unvarying menu of chicken wings, pop, candy, chips and cookies. Each year I wonder if this child's party will remain attractive to the maturing guests. In the fall of my son's senior year I was contemplating how to ask him without seeding his own doubts. Before I had an opportunity to say something, he came home and said, "Boy, the guys are already talking about the Christmas party. They want to make sure you are having the very same chicken wings." Some of that, I'm sure, was about boundless adolescent appetites, but I believe another part was also an expression of the importance of tradition and the allure of maintaining special connections.

Matt's inscription in his year book reflected the strong family connection he felt. In the Senior Parting Words section he reminded everyone to "Live, Love and Laugh," which has been his family motto for as long as anyone can remember.

Traditions such as the annual Christmas party or any others that occur with some regular sequence promise us that however much things change, there are some constants in the mix which tell us about the richness of being together, our shared experience. These personal traditions offer a sense of stability and security when everything else is in flux. The wonderful thing is that almost any repeated, pleasurable activity seems to hold this magic to revisit over and over. We need these things to balance us as we go forward with what we know are changing times, and later, looking back, they form the tapestry that tells us where we've been.

In all, being the parent of a senior is a once-in-a-lifetime part of their life and ours. There may be other siblings, but with each it is the only time for this expression of passage. It's kind of a merry-go-round brass-ring analogy. We need to reach for this one with all our energy, because even if we miss the brass-ring catch, we still need to have made the full exertion to help move this transformation ahead. Our earnest efforts help us, as well as the children, especially when looking back. If we feel we gave this period our best, it is both consolation and validation for ourselves as well as any enrichment we may have given our children. They may appreciate that we deeply cared and that our nurturing support at this time made a difference. Deep in our souls, we want this to be positive and memorable for the right reasons. We just have to persevere to bring our mindful awareness to this period as an experience that will resonate through time.

Be glad you had the moment.

⤳ Shagan

Home Remedies

- Despite our wish to do things jointly, there is an area that responds well to specialization, the "best-suited" parent doing what works best. Let one parent help with the details of college applications, for example. Pick the organized, detailed person. Fall of the junior year is not too early to begin.

- Find ways to use a parent's controlling nature. Rather than allowing a parent to take over, it can be beneficial to have the more structured parent make a list of what is important and to identify those areas that mean the most to him or her. "Would you consider outlining what questions you'd like to have answered by May 1?" may be a way to start a conversation. Then, "Maybe we can talk about how best to elicit those responses from our student."

- Know when to be quiet.

- Begin to loosen your hold gradually this year. Show the senior that you trust him to make his own decisions. It will be more comforting to you to watch him learn while he's under your roof.

- Lighten your own schedule. Now is the only time this person will be a senior. Promise yourself you can do it well because it is the only time. Do this only day by day so it doesn't get too complicated. Just today.

- Make time to spend time together, whenever you can steal it or schedule it. One father suggested breakfasts together because he knew his heavy travel schedule made him miss too many dinners.

- Recognize your own traditions. It is not the time to let them go. If you have always gone out to dinner on Sunday nights, ask that it be continued or modified to meet their needs. Preserve the idea.

- Get permission to open their college-application mail if they don't want to do it. "If this isn't open in three days, do I have your permission to open it? If not, how shall we handle this?"

- Have a plan to cope with your child's floundering. The time-honored technique of labeling what they're feeling works well here. "I can see this is very frustrating for you. Is there anything I can do to help ease the pressure?" Sometimes even that light question provokes a large "NO, I'M FINE!" In that case, you are better off labeling yourself: "If I were trying to sort through all this, I'd be overwhelmed." And, if all else fails, "Boy, this is hard!" Something to let them know you have some idea of what they're feeling and a name for it to show that you are plugged in and available.

- Hug your child.
- Make statements, which gather more information and move things forward more quickly than questions. Questions, particularly hardball questions, usually get stonewalled.

- If verbal communication doesn't work, open lines of communication via written notes or, my personal favorite, the "yes-no checklist." Use sparingly.
- Start researching e-mail options.
- Take tissue to graduation.
- Consider having a graduation party with a number of other families.
- Consider using a public place rather than home—swimming pool, park, community center . . .
- Consider having a party at the end of the summer, making it a good-bye party at a less-party-filled time.
- If time permits, be creative with graduation presents

    (named towels—the large, beach size with their initials or name—maybe with college colors; lanyards, preferably from their intended college; tool box; picture frames; little lesson-type books; phone cards; photos; personalized stationery; gift certificate to new college town restaurant; toys).

- Kids still like getting real gifts.
- Get out your own high school yearbook from senior year and see if you can reconnect.
- Laugh whenever you can. Deep, resounding laughs.
- Say "I love you" often.

II

When the Pie Was Opened the Birds Began to Sing

*Half the failure in life arises from
pulling in one's horse as he is leaping.*

━℮ Julius Charles Hare

Dancing in the Streets

he soft breeze wafting into summer takes us along for the ride. After the tumult of the senior year, we are expecting—maybe only hoping for—a respite from the travails of the recent momentum, but this would be yet another in the series of mistaken expectations. Or, hopeful wishes dashed. Our progeny's wish to savor the moment and extend the ecstasy, in the usual case, makes for more rather than less activity.

The turning point is the first graduation party, and make no mistake, this is a true celebration. It is a ritual full of the richness of their mutual reminiscing of how great it was laced with their expectations of how great it will be. They are as welcoming and generous as benevolent conquerors and thoroughly enjoy being together in a collegial, convivial way. It is both a celebration of the past and the beginning of this special summer; the party goes on. We move from early-June graduation to late-August good-byes and parents speak of never having been so tired in their lives. Three A.M. feedings were easier than waiting up for the late-night revelers. Barbara remembered that first summer before college. She would finally have finished the evening dinner, dishes, and shower and be changed for bed. The time would be about 9:00 P.M. She said, "What I noticed was that the kids were also showering. The difference was the kids were getting ready to go out for the evening, partying with their friends, seeing a movie, etc. The generation gap was very obvious to all."

The social-life changes are a symphony of fluidity. The structure of school is irretrievably lost, but something is needed to replace it. Those kids who thrive on contact often reach out of a former comfort zone to include others—the familiarity of previously shared experience, albeit indirect, overcoming the earlier reluctance to move outside the established social set. Others find themselves protectively narrowing their circle and solidifying their boundaries to answer the absence of the missing school structure. Either way, there is a change undeniably presenting itself and the graduates undeniably responding. Whether it is with few or many, one thing is clear: They seem to prefer to be with friends, or even alone, rather than with us.

In the extreme case, it seems they try to outrun the inevitable. One coach watched a graduate who seemed to make a personal vow to extract all the fun he could from his last summer at home. He thinks the boy would have done away with sleeping if he could have, just so he could spend more time enjoying his friends and his summer. He had so much fun every minute of every day that the coach began to wonder if with so many highlights it would be hard to say good-bye in September. If you are enmeshed in a constant party, it's hard to notice that the end of summer indeed approaches, day by day. Following Tom's departure, the coach said, "I am not sure that the way it worked out for Tom his senior spring and summer always makes for the easiest adjustment in freshman year, but in the long run, I think it makes for a better life." Many think kids who have a great spring of their senior year and summer are more homesick that first fall away because of the stark contrast in comfort.

If you are lucky enough to live in the summer-gathering house, you'll not only get to see your own child but everyone else's. It is the new carpool venue. You get the information as it drifts through the house and you may even have more dates and basic data relating to their college activities than do their own parents. The catch is, you also get the 1:30 A.M. phone calls from worried parents, the 2:00 A.M. phone calls from people still looking for the party, six unexpected guests in your home every night, and by midweek even peanut butter and jelly will look good in the cupboard because they're the only things left. Defensively, one family required that everyone reserve Wednesday night for a family-only dinner. When the phone didn't stop ringing at the first family meal, the parents then required that everyone meet at a restaurant Wednesday nights. The father was a little upset that he had to pay a bonus to be assured of a visit with his family, but their newly coined tradition has continued.

As if in a mysterious alchemical process, as awareness grows, denial increases. Parents unwittingly provide a release valve–asking hopeful questions about summer jobs, thoughts about fall, anything suggesting a push to end one chapter and begin the next. What parents need to know now is that there will be precious little verbal communication this whole summer. The kids are afraid to speak because speaking about something requires thinking about it. We are afraid to speak because we know we're in dangerous territory and something in this tenuous place might tip over. Again, statements rather than questions work better.

As the ritual progresses we become so attuned to the denial that it is easy to worry about form and forget what is substance. So we hint, prod, probe, suggest, and intimate in ways that feel like desperate whispers to us, and are received as confronting shouts by them. As always, we become the receptacle of fear, the targets of anxiety: They kill the messenger. Rather than struggling with letting go of a safe, familiar time, students can make parents the convenient problem. It is easier to argue about tonight's curfew than to worry about the unknown.

Not that these entanglements are merely ploys of substitution or transference. The pull away is real and earnest. Eighteen years of age means freedom and the closer it gets, the more practiced the empowered stance of our graduate-cum-almost-adult becomes. It's another definitive point along the continuum that began early in the senior year and has been carried along by the already surging river of completion cresting in late May or early June.

Swept along by the force of a senior year, which took on a life of its own, the graduate bounds into summer invulnerable or at least impenetrable regarding parents. We say eighteen years of age is adult standing, but it isn't, not really. Kids believe the opposite case, of course. Regardless of living at home, heavily subsidized by parents, they profess indignation, even belligerence toward daily communal living requirements. Basic courtesies–telling us where they're going and when to expect them home and regular family responsibilities–are all seen as impositions, interferences, and precious time wasters.

A single mom was exasperated by the increasing lack of help in maintaining what she thought to be only meager hygienic standards. She sought to gain cooperation by explaining that it wasn't she who needed help, the "house" actually did. Anywhere he would ever live, she wearily explained, her son would need to make beds, empty trash, and know how to fix at least one meal for himself. It was too late in the sequence. He would have to learn that elsewhere, because that particular summer he couldn't hear that kind of message.

This time of endings and beginnings brings out the adultlike copying. At one point during the summer when three friends were feeling their very best, DeAnne walked outside to see the her son and his two best friends lounging in the hot tub with their new cigars. It was the height of power. Lying back as if lords of the yard.

Watching them also brings us back to an earlier time and our wishes for what had been. A reflective mom talked about the things she would have changed had she had the chance to do the summer before her freshman year in college over again. "Having been a fat teenager, I would have made sure that the person I presented to the new people I would be meeting was a person I liked. I wish I had taken advantage of summer as an opportunity to change the things I did not like about myself."

Like Robert Frost's paths diverging in a yellow wood, this period is certainly where our generational journeys begin to part, ultimately, making all the difference. We're busy looking for a glimpse of our children and they're off hoping to discover themselves. In the process, the easy summer we awaited never arrives. Donna Damico recalls: "We managed to survive the school year and headed toward summer knowing that we were facing issues centered around our son's need for independence and the need to separate as painlessly as possible. I, of course, wanted everyone to be cozy and together and was silently horrified that neither one of our children chose to spend much time with us that summer."

This is the reality for most. Try to be available and able to enjoy your kids when you do get to see them. One way is to establish their responsibilities and your expectations. Not that they will necessarily be eager for this conversation. If your conversation time keeps winding up in conflict, try doing it in writing. Make lists. With deadlines. If you transfer these negotiations to lists, removing them as sources of conflicts, the time you do spend together can be less full of those contaminated discussions.

And, if all else fails, try the "yes - no" list again.

And this, too, shall pass.

Hi ho, Hi ho, It's Off to Work I Go

If all life's a stage and we are but the actors, the play becomes complicated in this watershed summer. After all, when one has been trying to extend the frivolity of graduation, the idea of structured drudgery–as in a paying job–can evade one's notice. It's easy, actually, from this point of reference.

Enter, then, the parents as dramatis personae on this same stage. Since we've been the ones attending to the ignored household issues and other seeming impedimentia, we try to find ways to introduce the topic of work without breaking the spell. It's our job and it is impossible.

Most students are asked to contribute financially to their college education and in that last summer the obligation becomes more real. The dichotomy is that the need comes precisely when freedom and hanging onto the glory command all of a kid's available energy. Many students must pay for their entire education. Some parents stipulate they'll pay for the education and ask the student to buy their own books. Most ask students at least to pay for their own fun. Unless parents have an airtight agreement ahead of time, the summer job is going to be a first line of contention. The battleground is ripe and rife with possibilities, such as:

- Job hunting. The basic premise is that to find a job, you must search for one. This takes time, meaning time away from more important personally enhancing endeavors.

- Looking right. Our shared wisdom is that you must look as if you had an idea about what you should wear on the job you want. Sabotage by attire is common, but sabotage by delay is rampant.

- Hours for work. They say that any job will do as long as they don't have to get up early, work nights or weekends, or work at a job site inaccessible to friends.

- Family vacations. A skilled negotiator might be able to pull this off, but it might also be another sign in the process that this time is over. At the same time we are strong-arming them to work, we also want them to join in this last real summer vacation and our urging can work against us. Long weekends may be a compromise and a better bet.

When a graduate was offered the perfect summer job, working the grounds of the golf course—fresh air, exercise, an hourly rate above minimum wage, and membership privileges to the club–he told them he had decided not to accept the position. It required a 5:30 A.M. start time which was not possible.

The job-hunting saga deteriorated as his parents realized nothing would work for this young man. The parents decided that he had determined his no-work policy as early as April. He knew he wouldn't make money. The parents knew they wouldn't give him any money. The ensuing standoff put the parents in a bad mood all summer.

When he finally decided to work for a temporary agency, his parents realized it had everything to do with availability to friends and nothing to do with the money or the experiences. This tactic was rather ingenious and creative, as it did recognize a priority and did manage to fulfill it.

Others try to find work to meet their upcoming needs only to find it more difficult and daunting than they ever expected. One enterprising fellow found the employment market in his city so flat when he approached that he pieced together gardening work many days and parking valet work many evenings, to make a whole job. He had taken employment seriously and understood that if he didn't make any money, he wouldn't have any money.

Even responsible students, though, can put off getting jobs that take too much time and too much commitment. The ensuing debate with frustrated parents provides the kids a welcome respite from internal confusion. This is a kind of divert-and-conquer game, a setup, to be sure, but one in which all parties play their roles in tacit complicity.

One of my desperate attempts to secure a place in my son's future plans was to organize a houseboat trip to Lake Powell. I had heard nothing but good stories about how families bonded on these trips and how peaceful and rested they were upon their return. I coerced my brothers to accompany us, thinking we'd be safe with favorite aunts and uncles. Besides, my brother Ron had a small houseboat, so I was counting on him to be the expert. I also allowed my soon-to-be-freshman son to bring along a friend. I was quite sure his polite friend would raise the average. We tried to schedule it a year in advance because of stories about how difficult it was to find a boat. It was hard, since in September of his senior year he had no idea yet where he'd be going to school or when school would start. We scheduled the trip in early August just to be certain.

What an absolute disaster. I knew from the moment we started loading the car that it was a mistake. The two college-bound boys sulked all the way to Grand Junction, where we spent the night. They complained about the accommodations, the company, the food, and the idea. I figured they were just tired. We left early the next morning for Lake Powell and it rained all the way there. Great start. Their complaining and sulking continued. By the time we got to Lake Powell, I was worried that, instead of securing a place in my son's future summers, I was assuring myself no more trips ever.

There was a brief reprieve when we put the Jet Skis in the water, but even that was short-lived. The boat was dirty, there were mice, the air-conditioning didn't work, the sound system didn't work, and it turned out no one really knew how to run the boat. That summer brought the highest water Lake Powell had ever had, leaving very few places to dock for the night. This houseboat was huge and everyone got tense when we took off and landed as well as in between. I found myself getting upset with my brothers if they spoke shortly to the boys–thinking that I had enough problems on my own without my brothers having to make things worse. I was just sick. When we docked and left the boat, I was incredibly disappointed and sad.

Lesson: Don't schedule a vacation too close to departure time. Both boys were leaving lots of friends and going to the East Coast. The trip sounded good in June but was a terrible idea by the time August arrived.

Parents and kids are both overwhelmed, each by different issues, but not talking about it. Not directly, that is. We don't do a good job of knowing what's happening with others when we're trying to keep our own heads above water. In fact, we do our worst thinking then. So, what goes on in many normal households is everyone emotionally dog-paddles to keep above the waterline, making it hard to notice what's happening to everyone else similarly engaged. It appears as many separate pieces. It feels just like exclusion and, when we feel excluded, we take it personally. We are rejected just when we are desperate for inclusion in the launching process.

Finally, we cross an invisible threshold and begin to panic. It is then that it becomes clear and we know it wasn't just our imagination: They are stalling. Unmercifully. Alarmingly. And we know with excruciating certainty how receptive they are to our suggestions. It seems that little short of a catapult will help them move ahead.

There is one situation where expression of this procrastination takes place by omission: the incoming mail. Whereas the days between college application and acceptance bring a distinct lack of mail from colleges, there is a constant stream from acceptance until departure. And, curiously, the rush to open in the former is contrasted with a reluctance to touch in the latter.

The mail addressed to parents is attended to with vigor and excitement while that addressed to the student often languishes unopened. We worry so about being pushy and hope the mail calls to them the way it calls to us. Hard as it is to watch it lie there, it is worse to have them take it away and never mention it again. Don't be surprised to find much of it still unopened the day of departure.

When a freshman left a phone message just minutes after his parents had dropped him off at school in the fall, they realized that many pieces of mail must have gone unopened. Medical forms were missing, signatures had to go Federal Express, and the all-important football tickets had to be ordered immediately. For the can-do parent, the choices get sticky. Of course, the can-do mother knew how to solve the problem and she also remembered being warned to suggest options rather than give advice. In this case the thinking process went like this:

Oh, no! He is upset at departure.

Oh, well, I've always thought natural consequences were great teachers.

But, I know I could whip this problem quickly into shape.

Could he?

No, not right now.

Should I? Followed by this conversation:

"How can I help?"

"I don't know."

"Would you like me to call?"

"Pleeeeeeease!"

So, he'll have other consequences. Mom decided he couldn't live with any more losses right then.

There is one exception to the kids' generalized approach to mail. For those being assigned a roommate, that particular piece of information is eagerly anticipated. It is even fair game for conversation. Many parents at this time describe their son or daughter agonizing over whom they might find themselves living with and frequently work themselves into a lather with worst-case hypotheses. It's a mistake to minimize these ruminations: I think much of the work of worry gets transferred to this category, symbolizing and holding all their terror about the unknown.

When Brian received his New Student Housing Survey, he was asked to describe his living habits. Brian had no problem answering the opening questions. He was a nonsmoking, late-night reader who listened to music while studying. He was asked to describe his living habits: extremely neat, neat, somewhat cluttered, or cluttered. He didn't want to be rejected or to live with another messy person so he checked neat. I believe that his extremely neat roommate must have wanted someone less compulsive than himself, because he also checked neat. Brian lowered the average of that duo but other good things about the match allowed them to function well together.

At some undetermined point, often in July, the importance of roommates hits and the students realize that a new roommate means a new room. Their room at home suddenly and unexpectedly needs to be cleaned. By them. Generally, in the early-morning hours. It is a forceful, determined, thorough cleaning, being a partial–nothing can yet be final, can it?–recognition of the moment at hand. It is metaphor put to elbow grease, it is the physical manipulation of destiny. Few things can be so easy or so difficult in the same moment.

One mother had made an early decision not to make an issue of the condition of her son's bedroom. Since it was downstairs off the laundry room, she just told him to keep his door shut, enabling her to do a pretty good job of ignoring the room. Just before he was going away to college, however, she told him she thought he really needed to clean his room and sort out all his "stuff." She offered her help.

They spent a whole day doing this, and although he didn't want to do it, once he got started, he was tossing things away left and right. She actually had to salvage some things she thought he shouldn't throw away. They ended up with many trash bags filled with his discards. "When we finished," she wrote of the experience, "his room was in an almost pristine condition, certainly one it had never been in before. He stood in the door of his room and said, 'This isn't my room anymore.' Oh boy! That just about broke my heart. P.S. That room never quite lost its smell of dirty sneakers and other boy smells, even after being recarpeted and painted!"

About one month prior to the college departures, three mothers mentioned that ironically all three of their college-bound children had cleaned their rooms that week. When Matt methodically packed his closet and emptied his drawers, his brother asked if he could use his desk while he was gone. He readily agreed. In the next breath he said, "I really don't mind anyone using my room, just make sure not to use the closet." Said Mom, "In our early-'70s-era home, the only thing home builders scrimped on were closets . . . this coveted space, and now I had given my word to leave it sacrosanct."

It is touching to witness, in the midst of all this cleaning and packing, your child signaling which items are most treasured. Some things are being packed up to be put away forever. Others are to be taken to college. But, some are to be put at the top of the closet to be looked at later. One of many, this, too, is a defining moment. How shall we know ourselves because of what things surround us? What to leave and what to carry along says much about becoming and about where we're going.

Ten Little,
Nine Little,
Eight Little Freshmen

Luckily for us, most colleges require that freshmen attend a summer orientation session. Many of these sessions include a track for parents, which may be the first time you get the true picture of just how minimal your role will become. It will also show you a rare side of your child: silence with their peers.

At an orientation session late in the summer, I sat at a table with four chatty adults and five nearly silent freshmen. One of the students was trying to strike up conversations with the other students and kept getting one-word answers. It was so hard to watch that parents started answering for their kids. I know we were all thinking it would be an extremely long, hard year if that silence continued.

Orientation is one of the summer moments into which reality slips, a small toehold that expands into a fully engaged awareness. Upper-class college students, chosen in particular for their skill in engaging with others, shower the freshmen with anecdotes about college life. They roar with stories of great camaraderie and offer a spirited introduction to their new world. Depending upon the tenor of the high school from which these new freshmen arrive, the mandatory discussions of topics such as suicide, roommate struggles, cults, rapes on campus, college-expulsion policy, drinking policy, studying, attrition statistics, and crime on campus deliver a new reality. It is clear that it is both an exciting and yet vulnerable time.

Most parents report that their experiences at orientation are wonderfully informative and tentatively reassuring. We parents show our own colors at this event. At my son's orientation in August, I watched as we all tried to look as if we were perfectly fine, thank you. But the truth trickled through. On the first day a mother and father walked into the first session. Dad took a quick left into the completely empty top half of the auditorium. Immediately and knowingly, Mom tugged at his sleeve with a half shake and half nod, indicating that there were seats closer and with other parents still available. He must have been used to that tug since his intended departure followed an arc, a small slump of resignation and recognition. Curses! Caught!

We were full of questions, many of which we knew we shouldn't ask. I truly believe that each of us was grateful and silently relieved when other parents asked the questions that revealed their own discomfort with letting go. One camouflage parents used was asking why, if they were paying for it, weren't they given access to everything? Several were worried that their students at that very moment were registering for classes and it was the first time that the parents hadn't been involved in the process. Other parents worried that their kids, who having come from small high schools with no computer registration, would be at a disadvantage. If we could only be of some assistance, just like always. Just a little.

We were given the opportunity to listen to sophomores tell their freshman stories to us, then later to hear from administrators relating their versions. I found the sophomore stories hilarious and yet sobering. They repeated examples of their own struggle to embrace independence and the tentativeness of those excursions into adulthood. They certainly helped us understand the other side of our needing to have access to everything. A realization dawns on most parents that one of the real blessings of the collegiate life for their children is parents having to know very little. It gives us practice for reforming our own lives as well.

One young man, Justin, talked about telling his parents he wasn't going to be a scientist like both of them. Another told of telling his parents he was going to be a teacher, knowing they would continue to hint at expectations to be more of what they had in mind–"Not that we don't want you to be a teacher, we think you'd be excellent."

Many of the students spoke of coming to college, excited and involved, but having great difficulty applying themselves. Parents were mesmerized and terrified. The sophomore who stirred up the most anxiety described getting "hosed" his first semester because he didn't realize that *no homework* didn't mean *no studying*. When he was quickly asked what a parent could do, he said "Hope the orientation leader tells them–but there's nothing you can do." I think we asked that question four different ways and finally gave up. Nothing we can do? About our kids flunking the first semester?

Other parents were trying to decide if their kids were at risk for being too involved or not involved enough. We spoke as though worrying would fix something. Our previous levels of control were being disassembled as we sat there. Thankfully our kids were in other sessions so they couldn't confirm their assessment of our difficulty in letting go. We wanted some clue as to how it would go and some assurance that it would go well. It was great help when one mother mentioned this was the fifth child she'd seen off to college. Awed, another parent asked how she got through it. "A combination of exhilaration, trust, and hope," was the reply.

The general message from parents after the orientation session, regardless of when it comes during the summer, is that we should expect nothing but stress for the entire summer. The fear of the unknown makes for tough days. However, do not expect to hear about orientation directly from the kids. It is astounding that most kids returning from freshman orientation tell parents nothing. They never discuss it again, though you can be sure parents try to elicit something. Every now and then a comment may sneak out but there will be no follow-up and you will be left to guess how it went for them.

One way we quell our anxiety is to get things organized. Sooner or later even the most reluctant student will find it necessary to pack, though the urge may come later rather than sooner. The new room and roommate assignment is really the catalyst for the next wave of activities, which seem to be gender specific. Perhaps girls are more accustomed to decorating rooms, but I heard more from mothers of daughters about this adventure.

Buying things needed for the new room is anticipated by the parent as a potential window of opportunity for basic communication. We would like to begin this as soon as possible but that is not a priority for the student. As we've come to expect, this activity represents movement, and movement is avoided. So, we wait. Again.

You may sneak your start by making a packing list. The top ten list from the male freshmen experts include:

1. Sandals for shower (cheap because the others won't dry fast enough)
2. Baseballs, Frisbees, basketballs, and other sports toys
3. Dry food for emergencies when the cafeteria isn't open: soup, hot chocolate, Raman noodles, macaroni and cheese, and dry cereal
4. Desk calendar and day calendar
5. Lots of sports clothing and casual attire
6. Effective alarm clock (you can't expect your roommate to wake you up)
7. Extra glasses (no one ever has time to put in contacts, even for a noon class)
8. Lots of socks and underwear (laundry is tough)
9. Quarters (lots of quarters–they become so scarce you can sell them 3 for $1)
10. Bring limited amounts of dressy clothes (you're more likely to dash to class in the T-shirt you slept in last night)

Lauren and Erin agreed with the top ten list but also needed: Windex, Lysol, Pledge and thank-you notes. They also wanted a long phone cord.

I've always appreciated the stories about mad scrambles to scrape together a year's worth of supplies in twenty-five minutes, with articles thrown into the shopping cart to get the job finished with as little thought as possible. One mom told of waiting for her son to give her the signal that he was ready to shop. She quit asking but, knowing his flight date, almost burst from the pressure of wanting to ask. Two days before he left, he rushed in and said, "I've got to get some things." No mention of why. They took off to the local bed and bath shop where he nervously tried to pick out sheets and towels.

She had waited all summer to help him through this rite of passage and he just wanted to get it over with as quickly as possible. He didn't care about colors, styles, or amount. Something to sleep on and dry off with. He was overwhelmed with the choices and seemed to become comatose before they hit the register. He rejected her suggestions that he get containers to hold clothes and possessions. He didn't want to take anything other than the bare minimum. Although she knew he'd need them immediately, it had to wait. This was all he could stand for the time being.

Parents of students planning to live at home and commute to college will miss the excitement (tension and trauma) of trying to help with purchases for a new abode. Even if you miss out on that experience, there will be other circumstances that will be brought to bear as variations on the theme.

For the student leaving home, the gathering of new accouterments and accessories is inevitably followed by the discussion of the physical journey. Now this discussion can no longer be postponed. It must be recognized if for no other reason than the obvious presence of the elements of the new life piling up ready to go.

This is all as it should be, but it can get crazy and leave us wishing for a "tilt" warning as on a game machine. A stressful time when everyone's pressures are slightly different, it's also one that we are all hoping to enjoy. Having a strategy for unplanned eruptions can keep you steady.

A young woman took her mother to task for, as she put it, "never teaching me to wash my hands after using the bathroom." Irrationality, it would seem, as in another case, when a neighbor told a friend that her daughter had been telling their family, "My mother cannot wait for me to leave for college." The mother was astounded since she'd been dreading the departure for months. There are all sorts of reasons that we see things as they aren't.

Other times you know exactly what's causing the flare-up.

One midsummer night I was feeling grateful to have my son John and his friend, Jordan, lounging in our kitchen. Before they left for the evening, Jordan asked John's younger brother, Mike, if he was planning to take over John's room when he left. We had carefully avoided that particular discussion—the more immediate things weren't going that well at the time. A sly smile crossed Mike's face and before he answered John erupted. "If he is going to take that room, tell me right now. I refuse to come home from college to a room I don't know. I need to know this minute so I can move to the basement bedroom tonight." Careful avoidance doesn't always work so well.

These incidents may seem inconsequential by themselves, but when put in the perspective of leaving home and the finality of one stage of life, they all demonstrate where young minds wander when the road ahead of them is so uncertain. You watch your children as they prepare to go off on the biggest adventure of their lives and outwardly they seem just fine. Soon you realize, when little incidents such as these surface, just how much their minds are churning and how preoccupied they actually are. Like the iceberg in the water with its greater reality hidden, the apparent is not always the consequential. And, yet, it is hard for us to know hidden and unspoken depths.

Every time you think there is a general behavior rule, something totally opposite presents itself. Shelly said, "I had heard so many stories from other parents about the senior year and the last summer home that I was really prepared for many battles. Instead we felt as if the time for our daughter to leave would never come and the stress of the good-bye was hard on the entire family. She attends a college on the West Coast that starts several weeks later than her friends. Watching her friends prepare and leave weeks before made her feel lonely and really increased the anxiety of the separation. This came out in so many ways.

"Between being accused of not helping her enough, to being thanked for making this college opportunity available, plus trying to finish all the chores on her lists and cope with my own feelings, I actually found myself looking forward to the process of getting used to her being gone. Of course, that was before I knew that I would walk around with a lump in my throat for several days each time she left to go back to school. I do remember laughing at her insistence on completing everything she had put on her to-do list. After shopping and more shopping for just the right pair of jeans, I finally told her that I thought there would be stores in Palo Alto that sold jeans, especially since it is a college town. She really needed to buy them here. She understood then, better than I did, that she would have so many new things to deal with that she needed to take care of all of the little details that she could now."

One summer doth not a freshman make. It is a mistake to consider summer a statement of how it is or to use it as an absolute prediction. If you think of this summer as your sampling of the new adult, it would be easy to conclude they won't succeed at anything. Something, fate or fantasy, usually intervenes and spares and saves us all. Looking to the metaphor of birds and nests, the young always fledge and move on. Perhaps that's why we are so fond of this analogy, it gives us assurance.

Just as there is a calm in the eye of a storm, in the middle of the summer, as the graduation parties wind down, the kids just relax and enjoy one another. Then, the hurricane hits as they prepare to send their first friend off with the beginning of the farewell parties. There's a totally different feel to these gatherings. It's knocking on the door that they don't want to open. They see themselves in the person leaving and in his experience.

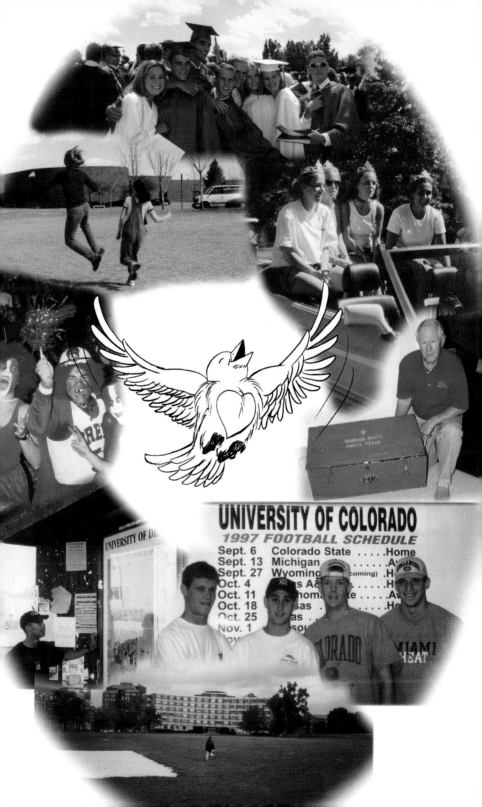

UNIVERSITY OF COLORADO
1997 FOOTBALL SCHEDULE

Sept. 6   Colorado State . . . . .Home
Sept. 13   Michigan . . . . .A
Sept. 27   Wyoming . . . (coming) .H
Oct. 4   . . .s A&. . . . . .H
Oct. 11   . . .homa . te . . . . .Aw
Oct. 18   . . .sas . . . . .H
Oct. 25   . . .as . . . . .Aw
Nov. 1   . . .ouri

My Real Parents

And They're Off

One father captured the moment of his son sitting on the lawn, with his friend, who was also going away. "He was being quiet like he almost never was. Sitting, not talking, looking off toward the mountains, contemplating the future, hazy and blurred and unknown as it was. Both going out of state, both going somewhere where they knew no one. They were leaning back on the grass, looking/staring at the sky–contemplating but not seeing the future."

The soon-to-be freshmen feel compelled to renew their commitment to having fun and enjoying one another's company as long as possible.

My friend Anne's son came home and woke her at 1:30 in the morning asking if she would allow him to have a party the following evening, a Tuesday night. She wondered why this was so imperative. As it turned out, the first friend was leaving for college in two days and no formal party had been planned. It was important to them to be sure and send their friend off in style. It was important to all be together. Months later her son is still able to name his friends in the order in which they left for school that summer.

There are departure days beginning in the early summer. Two young men left Denver, for example, in early June, both for military academies. Striking to those left behind were the new, strict parents, beckoning so early and with such force. Most students said they were glad they weren't leaving that early and tried to put that farewell experience behind them as quickly as possible.

One family with the honored gathering home was host to several sleep-overs as their daughter Robin's friends left one by one. Robin herself had planned a Sunday departure and had asked Kristin and Meagan to spend the night before for the final time. She got up early Sunday morning, bid them good-bye, and drove away with her mother. An hour later they returned to pick up a forgotten item and found Kristin and Meagan still sitting in their car in Robin's driveway dazed, trying to get over their friend's leaving.

The winds of change also affect the boyfriend/girlfriend rituals. During this stressful summer many relationships end, whether they simply cave in under the weight of the stress or because they are ready to be finished. Some mutually agree that handling a long-distance relationship would be futile. Other students find it desperately important to be connected with someone before their final departure for college.

When a freshman is still connected to an existing relationship there are diverse opportunities for worry for the parents. If the freshmen decide to go to the same school the concern is that they will not meet as many new friends and worse yet, commit prematurely. If they attend different schools there are many immediate problems: accumulating large phone bills, still not connecting at school because of loneliness, glorifying and fantasizing the relationship, and spending large amounts of money to visit the friend (often instead of visiting parents). Stand back.

When friends leave ahead of time, some of the waiting students get antsy. My own son, whose girlfriend left one full week ahead of him, spent hours on the phone to her in Oklahoma. When I had to leave town on Friday night and phoned home on Saturday, my family mentioned he had gone to visit his girlfriend. My heart leapt. He had packing to do and lists to complete and her school is ten hours away. Apparently they had decided to meet in the middle. He drove five hours to meet her half way, then drove home that night. Crazy. And, I wasn't there to worry in person.

At some point it is impossible to avoid packing. It may be the night before they leave. It is fraught with indecision and ambivalence and symbolizes the unknown journey ahead. It is also fertile ground for arguments. The lucky assisting parent would think reasonably that suggestions would be helpful. They are not. Once again, to consider what will be needed requires thinking about what will be. Some kids solve the problem by taking far too little, others by trying to take everything.

Anne spent a couple of days asserting that no one had matching luggage anymore and she would not be one to buck the trend. When it was time to leave, she gathered up her four black garbage bags and put them into the car never noticing the irony. Jason, a full-fledged slob by his own admission, had to have matching hangers when he packed. He even required that all shirts face the same direction. The attention to detail makes the big picture fade a bit if a small piece of it can be managed. Our sons and daughters may be almost ready to leave but the final move forward is a big one.

One mom said their trip to the Container Store was better than any reunion they could have planned. She said they saw every parent and child they had ever attended school with, from first grade on through high school. Some were crying, some were laughing, they all felt excited, scared, and ready to go. Their fifteen-minute outing to grab a couple of closet shelves turned into a touching two-and-a-half-hour trip down memory lane.

This is where lists come in handy, especially if they've been crafted by someone other than yourself, ensuring that you aren't doing the prodding or promoting. You aren't the commentator saying something is necessary or missing. But one mom commented, "I really think we could have packed in a couple of hours if we hadn't had those damnable lists. Instead we spent precious time alphabetizing everything." On the other hand, one college freshman said that a packing argument helped him see that his dad cared—he could see it in his eyes. Who is to know? Everyone's path is individual to them, their children, and their family dynamics. No part of it can be reliably predicted and we probably wouldn't want that, even though it might sound tempting on some days.

Sometimes things happen because they are supposed to; a dear friend's story illustrates how one man's caring at the right time at the right place brought about a total life change. Charles "Red" Scott, a Horatio Alger Award winner and a Genuine American

Entrepreneur, still marvels at how lucky he was to be able to go to college. In 1945, the leaving for college had a different air of privilege. Red grew up as Charles Scott in Paris, Texas. Although his mother and dad were intellectuals, they were not formally educated. In fact, his father may not have finished tenth grade. His family had little money and scholarships were very rare other than WWII veterans on the GI Bill.

After graduating from high school and a local junior college, Red had gone to work for the local newspaper, The Paris News, grateful to have a job.

Each town had its local World War II hero. Paris' was Billy Hart. Shortly after Red had taken the job at the newspaper, Billy came back to town before going off to college on the GI bill. He was honored with a parade down Main Street, then stopped in for an interview at The Paris News, where the few staff members were invited to meet Mr. Hart. When the publisher introduced Red, he said to Billy Hart, "This is Charles Scott, who was the president of his Paris High School senior class and now works for us." Red was elated to have such a lofty introduction.

A week or so later Red got a call at work from Mr. Hart, who greeted him with, "Hey, kid. Did I understand correctly that you were president of the senior class at Paris High School?" Billy then told Red that as senior class president of a AAAA school, he was automatically entitled to a scholarship to the University of Texas at Austin. He urged Red to check into it.

The next day Red went to his high school principal and relayed the story. The principal said, "No, I've never heard of that." Red asked if he'd check and the principal said that, of course, he would, but told Red not to get his hopes up. Two days later Red got a call from the principal. Billy Hart had indeed been right. Red was on his way to college.

When Red told his family, they were ecstatic. There was great singing and dancing in the front room of the Scott home that night. His proud father desperately wanted to do something special for him. He went to the Army Surplus store and bought a used WWII olive drab army footlocker. He carefully painted it bright orange with white stenciled letters, matching the University of Texas colors. He also drew a longhorn on it. The printing said: CHARLES SCOTT, PARIS, TEXAS.

Red packed up everything he owned and there was still room in the footlocker. As he stuffed it under his feet on the Greyhound bus en route to college, he was sure he was the luckiest man alive. His orange box has followed him through his long and successful career, assuming its rightful place of importance in each office along the way.

Red's simple financial philosophy: "As long as everything I own won't fit into that orange box, I figure I'm ahead of the game." To this day Red Scott remembers and honors Billy Hart for changing his life and thanks God for his good fortune.

Then it comes. We've put it off as long as possible, but the black bags and the orange boxes need to be closed. At the moment of recognition that this time is really over, we are all so full of feeling it is extraordinary. As in any truly important time, how we react is uniquely about us. Some kids start withdrawing early to try to make the leaving less difficult. Some speak of having no trouble leaving home, mostly when there have been difficult times preceding the leaving. Others keep up the facade all summer, then crack just before the leaving becomes inevitable.

One mother spoke of a homebody son who had gathered friends in his home for years. Leaving for him was going to be difficult since he had, perhaps wisely, decided to go to college across the country. The night before he left, she had to call him inside from visiting with his close friend and neighbor with whom he had been running nonessential errands for four hours. When he realized it was time to say good-bye and wrap up things, he unraveled. He sobbed, saying that he wasn't sure he could go if he felt this awful, and was worried about how he'd cope at school feeling so sad. It is at those times that we as parents have our work cut out for us–being able to support when we are allowed in and finding it necessary at the same time to be strong and stifle our own pain for the moment.

One sage, Gary Stollak, author of *Until We Are Six,* frequently says that children should be treated as guests. When I first heard that statement, I understood it to mean that we should treat them with the same courtesy we'd afford guests. Now I believe it to mean that we would like them to look back on their brief time with us and see it as comfortable and loving. We want them to want to return.

The best way out is always through.

∼℮ Robert Frost

Home
Remedies

- Make it the summer of lists.
- Have them submit list of rules they can live with.
- Try to get an agreement on summer jobs before the graduation parties wear them out.
- Give them a list of what jobs they have and how long they have to do them.
- Don't wait for the right time to talk about it
- Consequences of inaction—you can avoid doing laundry or buying their favorite foods or deny car use (if they don't own it).
- Set up amounts of money for everything ahead of time.
- Shop early and often when filling the college larder.
- Be prepared to forget lots of stuff.

- Be prepared for last-minute purchases, even those that will be far more expensive than you had expected.
- Don't buy the wrong-size sheets. Extra-long dorm beds are everywhere.
- Get ready for angry outbursts over the summer. It is easier to leave when you're mad. Ask yourself—what else could this behavior be about?
- Develop curfew strategies: Set the alarm for midnight. If they don't turn it off, they're not home. Ask them to turn off the lights or turn on the burglar alarm system upon return. If you awaken, you'll know instantly if they're in or not.
- Be prepared to let those who travel afar pack as though they're going down the block.
- Do laundry lessons at the beginning of the summer.
- Laugh more.
- Set up the student's checking/credit card account early so it is not new.
- Expect useless things to come home.
- Get e-mail and be prepared to learn how to use it.
- Vacations: Don't schedule them close to departure time and include friends if necessary. Long weekends are more realistic.
- Keep the routine.
- Laundry packets all in one pack (soap and softener together in one packet)
- Get under-bed containers which are great, but measure first.

- If your child takes a car to school, consider AAA and cellular phones to help you all feel safer.

- Most kids prefer laptops.

- Fridge/microwave combos are standard in some college dorm rooms. They're lifesavers.

- Hot/cold water dispenser rentals are reasonably priced and very convenient.

- Attend orientation programs. They're informative for parents, too.

- Quietly slip family photo or other small treasure into luggage.

- They'll ask for stereos, TV, CD players, video games, and VCRs. These are universal requests and they'll be resourceful in getting them even if you say no.

- Get them a subscription to the local college town newspaper to help them feel at home.

- Avoid "I told you so's."

- Say "I love you" often.

Simpler Lists

Bed & Bath

- Twin extra-long sheets (T-shirt sheets)
- Extra-long comforter
- Blanket
- Fleece throw
- Pillows
- Pillow protector
- Extra-long mattress pad
- Egg-crate mattress pad
- Bathsheet-size towels
- Over-the-door-towel rack
- Carry-all shower tote
- Wastebasket
- Soap and soap dish
- Hair dryer
- Bathroom scale*
- Shower shoes (plain flip flops)
- Bathrobe (if very private)
- Tool kit
- Sewing kit
- First aid kit

Electronics & Housewares

- Electric alarm clock (reliable)
- Phone and answering machine (if not provided)*
- Desk lamp
- Clip-on lamp
- Lightbulbs
- Fan*
- Extension cords (check college's requirements)
- Surge protector
- Flashlight and batteries
- Stereo, VCR, TV, video games*
- Computer and printer*
- Small refrigerator and microwave (sometimes included, combo available for rent)*
- Coffeemaker*
- Paper plates, plastic cups, forks, knives, and spoons
- Large bowl (to accommodate popcorn)

Basics

- Backpack
- Desk caddy
- Desk supplies: calculator, scissors, tape, ruler, paper clips, stapler
- Calendar
- Drawer organizer
- Bulletin board
- Dry erase boards
- Mirror
- Posters, picture frames
- Dictionary and thesaurus (even if in the computer)
- Trunk with lock, preferably to fit under bed (you'll have to measure)
- Underbed drawers
- Hangers
- Over-the-door hooks
- Hamper or laundry bag
- Iron*
- Quarters
- Soap and dryer sheets
- Family and friend photographs
- Large container of aspirin or other over-the-counter medication
- Box of Sleepytime or Fast Lane tea
- Copies of prescriptions (medication and glasses)

- Duplicates of all personal items (college towns are notoriously exorbitant)
- Mounting squares or Handy Tak to hang things
- Rugs*

Mark everything as though going to camp, just more subtly.

*Coordinate and check with roommates to avoid duplication of major items.

III

This Is the
Way We Wash
Our Clothes

*We must free ourselves of the hope that the sea will
ever rest.   We must learn to sail in high winds.*

⌐℮ Leif Smith

The Cheese
Stands Alone

 omewhere between late summer and late September, that longest journey transpires in earnest, the college-bound child taking off from the nest and flying away alone–often literally–to the beginning of a new life. It resonates both in spirit and in physical distance, and regardless of the actual mileage, is the symbolic closure of the preparation period and the start of a different life for all. It is the moment we knew would arrive. Perhaps we didn't really sense, didn't really want to sense, the finality of this instant: Nothing more is going to happen to get ready. There is nothing more to do. Everything is done and things are moving ahead, just as we've planned–or not planned–on chaotic momentum alone.

Usually, the feeling lands in our heart with a thud, weaves a tangled knot in our stomach, or fills our eyes to brimming. We cannot call it friend even though in our blurred emotional thoughts we want our children to be fully engaged with life and to find it on their own terms with the tools we have tried to provide.

The energy of leaving is inexorable. It reminds us of all the leavings we have endured, most tinged with sadness, and the recollection surges within us. This one is so close to our hearts and so colored by errant thoughts of what else we might have done, or said, or thought. We are left to wonder if it would sting this much had we done something different. Even as we ponder this closure, in almost the same breath, the scale tips. There is a miraculous balance wrought by a true sense of relief, with the hope that all of the planning will lead to something magic. Everyone writes his or her own story at this point with its own particular meaning.

My friend Irene related this lovely college farewell story. "Although my mother's formal education was interrupted by World War I (she was born in Poland in 1906) she had a high regard for education and made sure all of us went to college. Mother would say, 'Education is forever. A thief cannot rob you of it, nor can a fire destroy it.' However, when I was packed and ready to board a train for college, she tried to bribe me, the youngest of her children and the last to leave home, to stay. She offered to fix up the attic and decorate it just the way I wanted so I could have my own floor—with bookshelves, my own bath, wallpaper—all the stuff I had longed for all during high school. I think she knew that, once I was on that train, I was never coming back, except for ever-shorter visits. And she was right. She was not an emotional woman and I never understood the depth of her grief at my leaving.

"When my own kids left for college," Irene went on to say, "the house became very quiet and I wondered why I had complained earlier about the noise. That was the first time I understood my mother's loneliness. Now when the kids leave, I allow an afternoon or an evening to sit with a cup of tea or glass of wine and mourn for times that are gone and will never come again."

The migration that empties the nest is one of great divergence of style and emotional substance. There are some families that gather themselves together to travel forty miles to the nearest college and others in which one parent or both flies across the country to deposit their child at the new destination. There are kids who arrive independently on campuses from airports and train stations. Many freshmen recount tearful journeys, sometimes interminable ones. One young man remembered a big van, filled with his things, and everyone crying to his great mystification. There are stories of dads driving like maniacs, mothers being hysterical, dads trying to find a comfortable role, and mothers trying to find themselves.

The physical separation has begun and the freshmen are often ahead of the families, as they should be, because their adventure is just beginning. These freshmen are facing the confusing emotions of what happens next and what it all possibly means. Their unknown, after all, is larger than any of the rest of the family's. They may demonstrate joy and excitement or a more blasé approach, presenting a "cool" demeanor in the face of the unknowable (even if covering up something roiling inside). The latter may actually be more difficult for parents to deal with due to an apparently thorough detachment which bespeaks a dispassionate passage but, of course, which may not be that at all!

Depending on where the parents are in the emotional spectrum, most of the general behavioral choices of kids at this time are not so easy. Paula Carroll, a freelance writer in Maryland, wrote about the familiar saying "There are only two lasting bequests that we can give our children: One is roots, the other is wings." Paula said, "In the hand-shake and the one-armed hug of the father to son, in the lifted embrace of father to daughter, in the touching of hearts as mother holds daughter, in the tiptoed reach and clinging embrace of mother to son, parents give wings to their children."

She reminds us that, "Hand-holding days are over. Now understanding hearts provide support." She concludes her lovely article with: "Like a bird, the child was born to build a nest, to sing a song. Whenever or however parents give the gift of wings to children, a remarkable gesture of unselfish love occurs. Parents accept the end of an era in their lives. They trust that unseen, immeasurable roots will sustain the growing child. They hope to see an adult, contented with his or her own composition."

When the Goldy family's eldest son left home alone and traveled two thousand miles to college on the East Coast, the three younger children, ages ten to sixteen, stood at the airport crying. The youngest child, a boy, tried to console his older siblings and parents and said, "I'm sorry to see him go, I was just getting to know him."

Sometimes we think that saying good-bye earlier is easier. Whether it is or not, the ritual is every bit as important. After much discussion, Dan and Cheri's daughter, Sheridan, spent her final high school year in

Kentucky, remaining there after her parents' move to Colorado shortly before her senior year was to begin. After coming home the following summer, she was apprehensive about departing for a college in Chicago; all agreed the family would take her to school. The week before they were to leave, Mom aggravated a ruptured disk in her lower back, but she was determined to accompany Dad and the younger brother on this important mission: dropping the only daughter off at college for her freshman year. To drive from Denver to Chicago, they rented a big RV with a bed in the back because it was easier for Mom to stand or lie down than to sit for any length of time.

All was going well until they wound up on Michigan Avenue in downtown Chicago in the huge rented Winnebago with Dad trying unsuccessfully to stay in one lane and lots of angry drivers honking and using sign language. Sheridan was mortified by the whole event. The next day they went for lunch and Sheridan cried all through the meal, still questioning her decision to go so far away to college. Her family assured her that everything would work out and they all said their good-byes at the dorm front door. As they pulled out of the parking lot, eleven-year-old Scott leaned over the seat and said, "Well, I'll tell you guys one thing: I'm NEVER going away to college!" True to his word, he went to college forty-five minutes from home and loves both the independence of being away and the security that the proximity allows. P.S. Everything worked out fine for Sheridan.

There are pleasant surprises, too. Following the "what to bring to college" list to include picture of the family, the mother of a 220-pound football player framed and packed the perfect snapshot of the family for the dorm room. As they were unpacking, he laughed and asked her not to expect him to hang it on the wall. She said it was just for him to keep in the bottom drawer and look at only when he missed them. After the bed had been made, the parents decided to give him a little time alone before saying their good-byes and retreated to the campus bookstore to buy a school hat for his little brother. When they returned, the picture was proudly displayed on his desk. Their eyes met with a smile: no words were needed.

"As my son and I drove the forty-five minutes to school with his four roommates traveling caravan style," one mother recalls, "I felt we should set some parameters so as to avoid embarrassment. I asked him just exactly how we should behave when we got to his room, 'Do you want me to make your bed or would that be too much?' In an uncharacteristically quick response he said, 'It's fine, please make my bed. Maybe we can get the boxes unpacked, too.' "

If a parent has accompanied a freshman to school, it's surprising how helpful it is to have the school tell the parent when to leave. Charlie Mayer, in response to his mother's strong feelings, said he felt he couldn't get on with his life, with his college education, until his parents left. Much to our discomfort, that is a common response. Charlie recalls being in a student meeting with the deans while the university president addressed the parents. One of the deans who was speaking with the students said, "Well, we have to move on now. We have to invite your parents to leave." Spontaneous applause rocked the hall. At that moment they were ready to be on their own.

The president of Boston College, Father William P. Leahy, included the following in a welcome speech to his new students:

We will be learning together in the weeks and months ahead. I am grateful that you chose to be a part of our family. I suspect that some of you may be feeling a certain amount of anxiety, especially as you think about classes and academic requirements, meeting new people, and being away from home . . . .

Let me now say a few things honestly and directly about what we expect of you as students:

- Challenge yourself to learn, to stretch, to encounter ideas and people, to form yourself as an adult.

- Be disciplined, balanced students. You are here to first get an education, but relationships, campus activities, your own social life, and having fun are important, too.

- Treat other people respectfully and morally.

- We urge you to be mindful of your moral and personal responsibilities and of the consequences of inappropriate action.

- Be alert to any difficulties you may be having, and treat them earlier rather than later.

- Remember that life has a spiritual dimension.

- Take care of yourselves physically. Like your mind and soul, your body is a gift. Respect it. Be good to it.

- If you are not of legal age, and I know that the great majority of you are not, do not violate the law of using alcohol. And please remember that drinking to excess is wrong, whether on campus or off campus, whatever your age.

- Learn to be a citizen, be concerned about the society in which you live. Sooner than you anticipate, you will be asked to lead it.

That college president had his list of hopes and expectations written out in front of him. When talking about the good-byes at the dorm door, every parent has mentioned the overwhelming wish for one more chance to pass on similar words of wisdom, with a list in hand. All that is really needed at that moment, however, is "Good-bye and I love you." Then you can hand them your own list. For example:

Now, before you go . . .
Stay in touch
Tie those shoes
Buckle your seat belt
Be safe
Call home
No nonsense
Brush your teeth
Stay with the group
Wear clean underwear
Lights out . . .
Did you make your bed?
Say your prayers
Don't walk alone at night
Change your bed
Take your vitamins
Wear your coat
Did you do your homework?
Everything in moderation
Beer on whiskey, mighty risky
Don't put off until tomorrow . . .
Do unto others . . .
Cold for colors . . . warm for whites
Neither a borrower nor a lender be . . .
Drive carefully

Know your limits
Good night, Moon

Sometimes the reality that they are on their own is packaged for them, as above, and, occasionally it strikes through the famous effect of unintended consequences. Having been in Europe for World Youth Day in late summer, Bill missed his college's orientation. The timing was such that he had to land at Kennedy Airport in New York, take a cab to LaGuardia Airport, then fly to Ithaca, New York, without returning to his home in Denver before starting school at Cornell. His parents tried to discourage him from taking the trip, stressing the importance of orientation, the need to get to know other students, to be rested when classes began, and all the sorts of things parents would normally say. And, like a typical young person, he decided to go anyway.

It was a perfect trip until the return plane ride on which he and most of the others from their church became violently ill, presumably from food poisoning. He was sick most of the way across the Atlantic but recovered somewhat before landing at Kennedy. He spoke to his sister on the phone just before he picked up the cab to LaGuardia: "I'm sick, I'm tired, I'm in a strange city. I guess I'm on my own." While some students are safely applauding the departure of parents, others have a more independent epiphany to announce vividly to themselves.

At some point in this transition, it is clear to most that the parents are having a hard time of it all. Students repeatedly commented that they had very strong feelings themselves, albeit about issues different from their parents', and felt they had to withhold their emotions to protect the parents. They also candidly said that if a parent cried too much, they felt responsible for that parent's feelings. However, if parents didn't cry at all, they secretly wondered if they cared enough!

Like a snapshot recording a second, a parent reads the separate, small events of life. When the passage is difficult, we try to err to the side of being cautious. But in this strange dance, we can miss a good deal of the nuance by assuming the behaviors are much as they are in the usual case. So much of this journey is almost beyond vocalization. We hear, we feel, and we see things transpiring. So do they. It's almost as if it's always been this way, but here the messages are differently intoned, have a new context. Our ultra-carefulness allows us our own perception while we and they may be missing the larger, more complete composite. Perceptions carry us forward, even if it is snapshot by snapshot.

So off we go and there they are. Their need to connect and be a part of something is overwhelming. The first challenge is the roommate. Except maybe for overnight camp, few have had an opportunity to experiment in adjusting to living conditions with strangers. It is indeed the best and the worst of times.

Jacque and her mother had enjoyed spending a great deal of time buying sheets, comforter, big pillows, towels, etc., all very feminine and all matching. Jacque arrived the first day of school and made up the bed with the beautiful bedding. They decided to go out for lunch before Mom had to leave and while they waited for the new roommate to arrive. When they returned, her roommate was there, had done up her bed in army supply camouflage, and had draped army posters all about her side of the small room. Sometimes the fit isn't perfect. Jacque made the most of her first-semester experience, switched roommates for second semester, and life went on.

Although roommate stories are legend, dorm living in general has changed over the years. With coed dorms, it does seem that the kids who do not have opposite-sex siblings are at an extreme disadvantage. Girls are stunned at boy slobs and boys are totally mystified by female living habits in general. Adjusting to different habits is an eye opener. The trend now is specialized dorms. There are dorms with quiet rules, single sex, athletes, and some schools have even gone to theme dorms, such as academic or marching band dorms. One Colorado university is studying the impact of alternate rooms of different sexes on one dorm floor. During the first weeks kids are taken aback. After that it all becomes normal and, according to one woman, they start relating to each other as family members. Boys are notoriously more rambunctious in dorms and, even in non-mixed-floor dorms, having girls in the dorm seems to raise the standards of behavior. On mixed floors, an even more dramatic effect may be taking place. Boys simply behave better when there are girls around and girls don't hesitate to ask the boys not to trash things.

There are many obvious roommate differences: the odd-couple syndrome where one is a neatnik and the other is inordinately messy; one likes fresh, cold air and the other is always freezing; one gets up to the first buzz of the alarm, the other hits the snooze button for as many times as it will work; one needs seven hours sleep, the other gets by on four; one needs to study in quiet, the other needs constant music; one loves classical and the other ska; one is a day-time studier, the other a night-time studier; one has a computer, the other doesn't; one borrows and the other lends; one fills the larder, the other empties it; one does laundry, the other borrows clean clothes.

The appeal of rooming during freshman year with someone known versus an unknown poses a very complicated decision. At first blush it looks easier and more comfortable to room with a friend. It is rare, however, that it works as well as the experience of getting to know and adjust to someone new. Many students commented that rooming with a friend stifles growth. It is hard to really feel on your own or even feel free to reinvent yourself with a voice of the past so close. Plus the experience of that first year makes for more skill in selecting roommates during the remaining college years.

One freshman described an overly dependent roommate who had been a fine friend in high school. Later, when they lived together, she discovered that her roommate could never be alone. She felt smothered. Is there a kind way to speak one's mind and get the point across that things are not going well? How do you tell someone you feel smothered? Many of the first-year experience programs deal with these issues. At one orientation, the drama club addressed these issues through skits—they were silly and embarrassing, short and to the point, and the kids couldn't help paying attention. The common thread was that if you put off discussing issues, it would be too late.

When a friend's son was told by his roommate that the roommate was moving out, the boy was stunned. He thought things were going pretty smoothly; they weren't best friends, but they seemed to be getting along. As it turned out, the boy had been asked to move into his fraternity house a semester early. It was a great opportunity for the boy to fulfill his house requirements with the fraternity and save some money on room fees. Because the issue of moving had not been discussed and the roommate had not taken the time to tell the boy the reasons for moving, the miscommunication hurt the one boy and also left him with the debt of a single person in a double room. If the opportunity had been discussed when it was realized, another roommate could have moved in at the semester break.

Other differences work themselves out much to the surprise and delight of freshmen. When a very tidy, almost fastidious roommate was paired with someone who was able to live in reduced circumstances and who had developed a blind eye to squalor, both sets of parents waited nervously. Instead, both boys moved themselves toward the middle from the extremes. You just never know.

A common problem is the boyfriend/girlfriend roommate dilemma. You will find roommates sleeping or studying in the hallway or computer lab, or even physically relocating because a roommate's boyfriend or girlfriend is in the room. Three can be a crowd, especially if you don't like the visitor. Of course, it is better to find a way to discuss this before it goes too far, but that discussion usually occurs when things are truly awful rather than just slightly irritating. Those who are able to discuss it ahead of time come up with signals to indicate that they'd like some privacy.

Roommate relations also figure in another important aspect of dorm life: general freshman loneliness and homesickness. When lying in bed asking oneself, "What have I done?" "Should I have gone closer, farther, or to a harder or easier school?" "Is everyone happier than

I am?" roommates become the first line of defense against just this kind of malaise. It is oddly comforting to hear someone who is far away from home talking about not being able to go home more often, when the student who lives nearby needs to discipline himself to go home less. Then there are the wonderful discoveries–that a roommate knows about a subject that is absolutely burying you, that a roommate has friends because he lives close by, that a roommate knows how to do laundry. So many roommates get off to a rocky start only to connect over something small.

The kids need to address yet another dorm issue right away: the realization that one cannot study in the dorm room. Your handy alternatives list to refer to upon that frantic phone call after the first low grade could include study rooms, the library, labs, or a dorm dining room or cafeteria if available after mealtime. Emphasize that finding a quiet corner somewhere is critical.

One boy told of frequent trips home rather than weekends with a roommate who had a squeaky, smiling, stuffed big yellow bird on a spring hanging over his bed. The boy said he needed to study in a quiet place. Sometimes parents of students going to nearby colleges need to set limits on weekend visits home during that first semester. One university counselor suggested kids stay at school for at least the first month. She felt visits only once a month after that helped students establish a routine.

The laundry issue seems to be more of a problem for boys. Kyle explained his solution to me by using sheets as an example. You only have to wash once a month. First you put the sheets on. The next week you turn over the bottom sheet and reuse it. The next week you put the top sheet on the bottom and the bottom sheet on the top. Then that final week you turn the bottom sheet over. Very efficient. Another boy, Matt, commented, "To think I wore a clean shirt every day of my life–I even had choices of clean shirts." I learned that ironing was so shunned (unless there was a knowledgeable female nearby) that the boys routinely put shirts between or under mattresses to "press" them and call it a day. Matt's advice to boys leaving home for a dorm was to be sure to have plenty of good boxers. You never know who is going to be in your room when you wake up in the morning, you never know who is going to pull the fire alarm or at what hour, and, because their whole world is a locker room, it seems to be suitable attire.

In fact, boys were universally eager to talk about their laundry experiences. When we asked our German friend (and student) Jan to do some drawings, he asked what we had meant by the chapter "This Is the Way We Wash Our Clothes." I wrote back explaining the chapter to him. This was his reply: "Well, hey, there are about 15 different levels of clean clothes in my drawer. It's all a smelling thing. It ranges from 1, 'worn for 8 weeks'; to over 8, 'still good for a week'; to 15, 'perfect.' " He went on to explain that there is a system for determining the most economical use of clothes, a certain period before you get the cost out of restoring it, which is to say worth it to wash it. A level 15 sock, for example, would be more like a hammer. You could put it upright in a corner after peeling it off.

Scary laundry stories aren't limited to boys. One girl said she was sure to have a twenty-one-day supply of socks and a twenty-one-day supply of underwear. Laundry every three weeks was enough for her.

The mom of another freshman said, "My daughter comments frequently about how much cleaner her clothes feel when I wash them. Laundry done by mom is an unexpected pleasure of being home and my way of pampering her when she's here." The laundromat is one of the first places where creature comforts formerly taken for granted now begin to loom ominously. The second may be the cafeteria.

Some colleges boast good food, but it would be hard to compete with home cooking when expectations are heavily overlaid with other longings. Again, creativity is the norm. At schools with a food card, boys frequently hover around girls who generally eat less and make cafeteria friends from whom they can mooch food. One reason parents are welcome is because the kids know they'll get a good meal off campus or that Mom will bring a family favorite. There is also the ever-present "freshman fifteen," where despite claims of nothing good to eat, both men and women tend to put on pounds that first year. Of course, the standard rules of good dietary choices, with lots of variety and exercise apply as they do throughout life, but helping the kids from afar is not the easiest task, let alone your task now!

Other first-year traumas include what could be the common cold or double pneumonia, strep or mononucleosis. My son agreed to meet me in New York for a quick weekend. When he showed up Friday night, it was clear that he had an ugly respiratory virus and its consequent resounding cough. Our Saturday night was spent with my going out to round up chicken soup, McDonald's French fries, and a Ben and Jerry's milkshake for him. When I put him on the plane very early Monday morning, he promised to go to the infirmary as soon as he got back to campus. When I spoke with him Monday night he mumbled something about having gone in but having to wait until the next day for treatment. I knew it was urgent and, overcoming my reluctance to be an intruding parent, called the night number. The nurse asked me to call back in the morning– saying that he had probably gone to the main infirmary since she couldn't find his name on the roster.

At 5:00 A.M. (mountain time) the next morning I called and talked to a wonderful nurse to whom I explained that even though I knew she couldn't reveal any information because of privacy rules, I was concerned that he was at risk for respiratory disorders and didn't really understand the procedure there. She looked it up and informed me, much to my chagrin, that he hadn't been in! I was embarrassed and wanted to end the conversation as quickly as possible, but she saved me by saying, "I'll call you right back." In three short minutes she phoned to describe the conversation which had transpired. She had called my son and asked him when he was planning to come in. He said three o'clock. She said, "That's not soon enough. I have worried parents in Colorado, and you sound terrible. Get up and come in now." And he did. And I love her for all of it. When I asked him his first summer home about that intrusion, he said he didn't really care that I had called, but that 7:00 A.M. was way too early for her to call him!

When long-time and favorite teacher Marie Vachon called her grandson on his birthday, she was informed that five of the boys in his college dorm room were sick. She told them the story of the origin of spring break. Apparently so many children were absent from the schools when the seasons changed from winter to spring that administrators were forced to close the schools and disinfect the buildings. They gave it a week. As the boys' spring break was still three weeks off, she said, "You're going to have to open all those windows and scrub the room from top to bottom." They used an entire bottle of Pine Sol and a spray can of Lysol to try to disinfect so that they could get well and go back to class. Had the mother rather than the grandmother told them to clean, would they be well today?

Parents often have trouble allowing kids to discover things on their own and trusting that they'll figure it out. On the other hand, the common expression from freshmen across the board when their parents were driving away was: "What will they do without me there? How will their life be different without me?" They are beginning to sense the void they have left in their parents' lives and are also beginning to see their own separateness.

Rock, Paper, Scissors

Shortly into the fall of the freshman year, questions about the details of living on one's own begin to pile up on students. When the initial panic dies down and they move beyond having little things paralyze them–they can find their way to class without getting lost or know a person or two to whom they can confidently say hello–their anxiety is freed up to roam into other territories. They begin to miss the comforts of home and allow themselves to think about it. However, they do not call it homesickness. At a recent Boston College orientation, the administrators told parents of a decision to offer a Homesickness Group to the 2,000-plus freshman class.

Absolutely no one signed up. The counseling center, however, was flooded by kids who had seen the announcement. They didn't want a group and weren't homesick but wanted to talk with someone about how they were adjusting. For a short time the center ran the ad knowing no one would come. They let kids know through seeing an advertisement for a group, that it was okay to talk about how it was going, even if not okay to feel "homesick."

When it is acceptable to label it homesickness, it gets translated into comments about weather. Shelly got a call from her daughter who called Mom at work. In a barely audible voice she said, "We are having a rain day. I'm sooo homesick." Apparently this was even worse during the second semester. Homesickness is a natural progression and can't be avoided. It comes in spurts and is relieved temporarily by a phone call. Like the changing seasons, the students move gradually into their new lives.

Repeatedly, it is said that the two most common problems freshmen present at a counseling center are a pet dying or losing a bedroom. One boy said. "It is hard to believe they miss you when they turn your bedroom at home into a study." Most experts advise keeping a bedroom until at least that first visit home.

One large and complex area of difficulty is relationships, whether at home or at school. The kids take them very seriously. Parents need to take them seriously, too.

When the freshmen are feeling desperate to belong, they choose friends quickly—with lightning speed, in fact. They glom together and develop instant friendships to accommodate that need to belong. Some merge into the traffic gently, while others find it easier and faster to connect. Regardless, the speed of connections needs correcting somewhere during that freshman year. They begin to know that they'll eventually find friends. They get more selective and begin to weed out and find where they belong.

Not only are they working at getting comfortable with friends, living conditions, and time management, they now have the opportunity to become acquainted with the system. Money makes the system work, but money isn't simple. There are credit cards, debit cards, ATM cards, checks, travelers checks, credit card checks, debit transfers to the checking account, phone banking, on-line banking, drive-through banking, and cash. No wonder the kids struggle so with it. One college financial administrator tells the story of a distraught freshman coming into his office to discuss his chaotic checking account. When the administrator told him he was out of money, the freshman said, "How could I be out of money—I still have checks!"

Another girl, Ginny, spoke longingly of her friend's arrangement with her parents. "They sent her $20 a week in cash. They didn't bother with a bank thing. True, toward the end of the week it could get tight and I could lend her a buck here or there. It was consistent. She knew how much she was going to have every week. She knew she had to ration it." Ginny thought sending a kid away to college with a new checking account and an ATM card was a mistake. She recalled the first time an ATM machine ate her card. She cried because she wasn't able to go to Taco Bell. Her father originally put $700 into the ATM account and that was supposed to set up her dorm room and buy books. She said, "I went through more money at school than you could believe. I have a problem with credit cards—they don't seem like real money to me."

One girl went home for a weekend early in the school year, and her father casually mentioned that if she bounced one more check, he would bounce her right out of the school. She had no idea that the checks cleared that quickly—she thought she had plenty of time for the transfers. One mother's first letter from her son read *Dear Mom, I got this in my box today, I saw money was due and thought I should get it to you right away! Love, Mike XXOO.*

When a boy phoned his mom and asked her for money to buy a reference book, she asked where his money had gone. He explained that he was very confused with the ATM card, the checking account, and the credit card. He felt he should let things quiet down for a bit so he could see where he really stood in all the transactions. Because she gave him quite a bit of money every month, she was surprised by the call and calmly asked how much he needed for the book. She was surprised when he said, "Fifteen dollars." She was sure it was going to be an expensive encyclopedia update. Unfortunately, at this point he couldn't even be sure of the smaller amount.

Cash-flow issues are intrinsically tied to the phone-call schedule. We do hope ours is one of the numbers on the phone bill and it helps to be prepared for fewer calls than hoped for or the dreaded crisis call. Most suggest that once a week is a good plan for calls—Sunday night works well. It is nice to know the weekend is over and they're okay. You can never tell without asking what they'd like. Let the freshman set the pace.

You may get an urgent call for which you find yourself unprepared. It may be as benign as "I hate my roommate;" "I wasn't invited into the fraternity;" "I have three papers due tomorrow and I haven't started any of them;" "If I don't get an A on this next test, I'll probably fail the class;" "The food here is terrible;" "I have no money left;" "The library doesn't have this book and I need to read it by Monday." Or the ones you're really not prepared for: "I miss you," "There has been an accident," "I've been hurt." Nothing will prepare you for these. To the others, your response of "Oh, boy! That's a tough one! What do you think you should do?" will get them to talk and probably come up with some good solutions on their own.

One mother's response did the trick in an instant. Her college freshman looked at her schedule for finals and found all five to be on the first day. She knew she was in trouble. The night before the big day, she panicked, and called the most practical person she knew for support. Knowing her mother would talk some sense into her, she called in tears and said she couldn't do it: five finals in one day. She waited for the calm advice. Her mother immediately responded with, "I'll be right there to get you." Taken aback, the daughter said, "No, you are supposed to tell me I certainly can do it and I've done it before, and it will be no problem."

In any case, you have to be ready to listen. More than likely (but not always) they have a solution in mind and just want to vent. Don't give advice. Don't give your solution. Ask how they're thinking of handling it. Ask how you can help. Reflect back to them what they're most likely feeling, as in "that must be difficult," or "I'm sure that is frustrating." It is fine to say, "I'm not sure what I'd do if I were you." But, forty miles away or four thousand miles away, it is not likely we can do anything. Regardless, it helps to have someone you feel you can call. And, yes, some kids will always have to learn things the hard way.

Some parents, too. Greg finished his freshman year with good grades and few scars. He announced he wouldn't be going back in the fall. His parents were confident that this was just end-of-the-year stress and hoped that after a couple of weeks, things would look brighter to him. The summer flew by and he repeated, "I'm not going back to that school. I really don't like it." He reluctantly went back because by that time it was too late to apply to other schools. But, he couldn't handle it. He was home after a couple of months, no school to go to, tuition money paid and nonrefundable, a semester behind–a tough lesson learned for both Greg and his parents. Perhaps he learned to be more assertive, and the parents learned to listen more carefully. Shortly after, he was accepted to another school for the next semester and, after working for three months, was looking forward to continuing his studies.

Sometimes we listen too carefully, as illustrated by Jena, who called her mother in a panic right after falling and breaking her toe early in the fall of freshman year. She told Mom that it was broken and that the infirmary had asked her to stay off it and wrap it. Mom and Dad worried into the night. When they finally called their daughter the next night to ask how her foot was, she replied casually, "Oh, it kind of hurts after all the dancing. I put cotton around it and borrowed extra large tennis shoes, then we went to the dancing place by Tijuana." From then on the parents decided that every story would be a funny story. "Don't worry about us," Jena's mother told her daughter, "because we know now not to worry so much about you."

Some of these hard conversations make e-mail even more appealing than it already is. It turns out that e-mail is a lifeline. Parents will learn to appreciate e-mail but the student learns first. Countless hours those first three months are spent trying to locate old friends and connecting with them to compare stories. It isn't as official as a phone call, and desperation doesn't show quite so obviously. This is true for parents, too–stay tuned.

When the unfamiliar begins to become familiar, when the student knows where to buy Pop Tarts and toothpaste, or where to get a haircut or do laundry, college starts to become home. But not home home. When my son called telling us he was looking forward to Thanksgiving, I e-mailed him back telling him we were really looking forward to his visit. He flashed back an e-mail telling me it wasn't a visit. He was coming "home." That was the last time we used "visit." I felt particularly lucky that in the e-mail before Christmas, he was even telling us that thinking about the aforementioned disastrous Lake Powell houseboat trip made him nostalgic.

One seventh grader went to visit his brother at school for a weekend just about a month after school started. He felt very much at home. He commented, "Everyone at the college seemed to know my name." He had been introduced by his nickname, Sfuz, and even when walking across campus, students who were walking along looking at the ground would look up, smile a broad, welcoming smile and say, "Hi Sfuz!" The older brother commented that Sfuz seemed to know everyone and, in fact, more than he himself knew. At spring break, when it was acceptable to talk about those things, the younger brother commented that the guys didn't seem to be talking to each other much that first month and he felt like a welcome distraction. Something like having a cute dog to break the ice and to use as a conversation opener.

Having siblings visit can also be a great reminder of family significance. A friend wrote that the freshman year had been a combination of pure excitement and homesickness. My friend and her husband sent their twelve-year-old to visit her sister at college for the first time. The freshman said, "I didn't know what I was missing until she walked off the plane and stood in front of me." The younger one was greeted with hugs and tears.

About the beginning of October the stretch between the first day of school and the first vacation looks extremely long. College counselors report this time being rife with homesickness. Many students report, however, that when they get home and go through the initial exciting stages of reconnecting, they come to know that they have a routine somewhere else and frequently have difficulty knowing what to do with themselves. They had talked so boldly about returning home, and after having experienced such freedom on their own, they quickly chafe at the old structure.

The structure of that long Thanksgiving weekend seems to be each freshman trying to connect with as many friends as possible. It is a mad scramble and by the end of the weekend everyone is exhausted. If the freshmen were expecting life not to have gone on without them, they are sorely disappointed and voice such to parents and friends. Sonny, expecting that his room would have been left a shrine to him, was saddened, then angered to find his sister had moved her clothes into his closet. Greg had trouble being civil to his younger brother who had moved in and changed the room beyond recognition.

Ellen Goodman wrote a entertaining article for the Boston Globe entitled "Tips for Returning to the Nest." It included such fine points as: In their months at college they have developed the life style of a roommate rather than a family member. She implored them to remember that roommates can engage in deep conversations about the meaning of life at 1:00 A.M. Parents cannot. On the other hand, parents think you look sweet when you are sleeping. Unless it's noon. She reminded us that we are learning to be a part-time family. Her final thought was in the form of a P.S. There's only one difference between roommates and parents. You can always get another roommate. P.P.S. This would be a good conversation to have with your freshman.

Each time families get together, there are new lessons. A powerful one comes from Parents' Weekend. The timing of it varies from a rather early one month into the school year to February. Regardless of when it occurs, it is significant for all involved. Some students talk about being sure all the other freshmen felt comfortable and were sharing that joy with their parents. If the weekend comes too early in the freshman year, the students are not at all settled and find it a double burden to try to accommodate parents as well as hang onto preliminary friend connections at the same time. At an early October Parents' Weekend, my son told me he knew he wasn't comfortable enough in the new environment to spend time with me and let the new friendships wait. Students were wishing the weekend had come later in the year so that they could have enjoyed both the parents and the newfound relationships. On the positive end, the first good meal off campus came sooner rather than later!

If You Study,
It Will Come

When the fluttering diminishes, the real task of college presents itself: making the grade academically. One student talked about having been to a prep school, knowing he was ready and finally getting to a place that would reward him for all his preparation. He was amazed to find what he considered to be no homework. The teachers were great, they handed out a syllabus, and it seemed to him that there was nothing to do. He recalls remembering the date, October 17, midterms, and flunking. Again the realization that *no homework* didn't mean *no studying*. It was the time when he and many figured out the "Oh, so this is different!"

One freshman who had won math awards throughout middle and high schools took an independent study in Business Math. Organizing his own time became imperative. He saved eighteen tests until the last two weeks of school, which made achieving even a C almost impossible.

Another bright young man had an overwhelming need to show everyone just how smart he was. He spent so much time memorizing the answers to the questions in Trivial Pursuit that he flunked out of an Ivy League school. Lindsay took a course in her major the first term. She got a "solid F," which made it impossible for her to continue in her chosen program. It is mind numbing to contemplate how long it takes to bring up a grade point average when it collapses under the weight of an F. I am sure she won't get any more Fs, yet, we ask why many have to learn the hard way?

When the kids dig in, the parents may be hearing from them but they may not be hearing what's worrying them. The first conversations seem to be about activities and what everyone is doing. Several commented that they imagined (correctly) it would be hard for parents not to have them as a part of their lives. I think it was also a projection about how difficult it was not to be a part of their parents' and families' lives. The freshmen talked about reflecting back on their old friends, wondering what they were doing, what the weather was like at home, especially if the new climate was very different. They were keenly aware of the parents' activities to try to stay connected. A few students remarked that their parents had even subscribed to the college newspaper and/or the local newspaper from the new locale. Only one woman voiced concern about all of this since parents quizzed her on the doings from the information they gleaned from her college newspaper.

Life circumstances offer insight into character. When one super-star sportsman and academic gave up a four-year college scholarship to one of the top four schools in the country after just one semester, most people were stunned. As he sat in the gym explaining the difficulty of distance as he faced an illness in his family, it became apparent just how big his heart was. How troubling to be so many miles away when you feel you can help at home. He certainly didn't give up an education; he just found a way to make it all work: a strong school, close to home, with a program in his sport.

When Barbara and Bill visited their oldest child at college for the first time they "were amazed at the beautiful campus, gorgeous trees, fall foliage. During the tour our son provided, we stopped at a high bridge overlooking a treacherous gorge with jutting rocks and rapids down below. He told us that in just the first six weeks of classes two students had thrown themselves off the bridge and ended their lives in suicide. I was devastated to think that what I thought was the wonderful experience of college could be so stressful as to cause someone to end a life. As I stood there looking down upon the river I told my son that if things got so bad that he would think about this bridge, he was to come here, throw all his books off the bridge, and catch the first flight home. We all laughed, but the message was clear–nothing was that important."

No one wants to hear the grim realities that are possible in new living situations. Although students hear stories during orientation, and most colleges give introductory remarks about possible difficult situations, being there gives them a different perspective on these issues ranging from roommate problems to suicide. There are assaults, robberies, alcohol-related problems including alcohol poisoning, automobile accidents, date rape, cheating, voices of hatred, hazing, seductive credit card offerings and the resulting debt, illegal drugs, and sexually transmitted diseases. It is smart for parents to be aware of these issues, too.

Freshmen proclaim feelings of invulnerability to troubles. It is critical, though, that they know these things happen and that they be prepared to take care of themselves and even help others in tough situations. On his second laundry visit home, Zach's mom froze as he sprayed Shout on bloodstains on the leg of his jeans. Assuring her it was not his blood, he told her the story: A friend of his heard screaming in a parking lot, ran to the car, realized a girl was being raped, saw the locked car door, grabbed a rock, broke the car window, and cut his hand in the process. The man in the car got out, giving the girl a chance to escape. Zach and a friend walked up at this point, saw the man running, and rushed the injured good Samaritan to the hospital where he was given thirty-seven stitches in his hand. It is unnerving to hear these stories and to know our children may be faced with such disturbing situations, especially since only a few months ago they were at home being protected by their parents. Suddenly they are at school and if a friend is crying about being raped or other traumas, they feel woefully unprepared. We have to trust and hope that they will react in everyone's best interest, and it is wise to remind them that there are always counselors at the college to assist.

At first, learning the road map at college is so overwhelming that it takes every waking moment. Gradually a routine presents itself and things settle down, so much so that freshmen may find they have immense spans of time on their hands, especially if they aren't working during the school year. Compare that to high school, where the day begins at the latest at 8:00 A.M. and goes for seven hours. Then there are sports, senior activities after school and at night, and that final flurry of all-day and all-night action right at the end of school. At college it is a shock to have fifteen hours of class a week and apparently nothing else. It looks as though they have forever to get things finished. Managing their time is more than knowing how to get lots done in little time. It is also knowing how to get something done in lots of time.

143

Eric, an honors student who did not seem to be very outgoing, went out of state to school. His parents were worried about his shyness and his mother asked if he'd consider being more social in order to connect. She wasn't so worried about grades—more worried that he would not fit in socially. He got into a dorm of 1,300 next door to another dorm of 1,300. First he became a floor representative, then dorm representative. Then Mom got a call—"You'd be so proud. I was elected dorm representative to the two-dorm board." So far so good.

However, be careful what you wish for. At the end of his freshmen year, Eric had a .009 GPA. In fact, 30 percent of the freshman class was failing and the university offered a select group of them the opportunity for a strict remedial program the following fall. During the summer Eric had to take a class in study habits, which he had to pay for himself. When he returned to school, as a part of his new program he was required to speak to the incoming freshman class about how big a hole he had dug for himself. In fact, he made that presentation to every freshman class until he graduated five years later.

Again, there are no easy answers. Parents worrying that their kids are too shy often discover a child who loves the social life in college. Others with gregarious kids worry that no studying will get done. One thing can be certain: If a student is doing "too well" academically, you may want to inquire about your freshman's social life. Connecting is crucial and it takes time to find the balance between the social and the academic.

There is much good news. Parents can relax because the kids do figure it out. The changes that seem so abundant and overwhelming to the parents are what give students substance and character. It is amazing how many issues they wrestle with, then resolve daily. Robert Cormier, in *A Bad Time for Fathers*, said: "You bring up your children to be self-reliant and independent and they double-cross you and become self-reliant and independent." Throughout the freshman year it is important for parents to savor every opportunity to affirm their student's growth.

A knowledge of the path cannot be substituted for putting one foot in front of the other.

— M. C. Richards

Home
Remedies

- Honor the separation but preserve the connection
- Practice how to react to troubling phone calls— "Sounds like trouble. How are you going to handle it?"
- Call without an agenda.
- Try to respond to the form of their call, not the content.
- Know that when they call home they want to feel snug. Try to be patient even when you're on your way out the door.
- Find a substitute word for homesick.
- Be available without hovering.
- Ask ahead of time what they'd like from you when moving in.
- Get e-mail—learn how to use it.

- Brace yourself for the changing of majors—the average is three, just so you know.
- Find your best calling night, usually Sunday, and ask how often.
- Be prepared for a last-minute purchase you could have found at K-Mart for almost nothing.

- No "I told you so's."
- Order the college town newspaper for your student.
- Encourage the return home of useless things.
- Know a roommate's/friend's name and roommate's parents' names and numbers.
- Make that first birthday or holiday away from home a fine one. Parent organizations help lots.
- Before switching around bedrooms at home, wait until the first visit and hope it will be their suggestion.
- Laugh often.
- Say "I love you" often.

IV

Empty Nest...

Full Heart

It is the privilege of adults to give advice. It is the privilege of youth not to listen. Both avail themselves of their privileges, and the world rocks along.

—e D Sutton

We'll Leave the
Light on for You

he beginning of the longest journey
signals the beginning of the ritual of
the good-byes. They come in many
shapes and sizes, singly or in groups, quietly or full of
exuberant backslapping. One poignant description of a
good-bye was related on CBS's Sunday Morning by
Richard Meier, the architect of the Getty Center. He was
leaving after twenty years of working on the Getty's
creation, construction, and launching. The interviewer
asked him, "Do you miss a building when it's finished?"
Meier answered, "It's much like taking my son to college.
The closest analogy I can think of is having your child
leave home. And that's why I enjoy those few precious
moments when I'm here and no one else is here and I can
walk around and say good-bye to it." Whatever form the
good-byes take, they are the necessary next steps toward
the new life.

The night before our son left for college as we sat in a circle with our arms around each other, our youngest, Michael, was dismayed and somewhat confused about this display of emotion that we had all kept under wraps and under control in the days and weeks leading up to the departure. For us it was a passage that we knew would and should come but which we emotionally regretted. We found ourselves thinking about how fast the eighteen years had gone. The years merged—from his birth, to playing soccer, to the years when he seemed to grow an inch a month—high school where you lost track of him during the day, to the weekend when you encouraged him and his friends with Sega/videos/games so you had a sense of where they were. At that moment we were overwhelmed with the enormous change that awaited him and us.

I watched a friend who was chatting with her daughter about the impending future ask, "How far do you think you can spread your wings?" Her daughter put her arms very close, tight to her body, and flapped just her hands very gently. Mom took hold of her arms and helped stretch them out and suggested, "How about this far?" Thus begins our own journey of letting go while helping them negotiate their own passage.

It would seem that anyone who has had a child can relate to their leave taking. A departure for college is surrounded with much fanfare and tradition but their moving on in any form signals powerful changes for all. One woman said that the trip to college was tough, commenting, "You prepare them for this and when they do it, you are upset because they don't need you." We try to embrace the moment tightly and find it hard to remember how eager we had been to be with our own peers.

Each family finds its own path. Parents work at being supportive, encouraging, and optimistic despite their life circumstances. And, even in ordinary circumstances, we find ourselves asking last questions about our competence as parents. Did I do enough? Am I too revealing of my own feelings about this transition? Am I doing something that makes my son or daughter feel responsible for my feelings rather than free to fly away on their own journey? How can I truly allow my excitement to show when it is so closely mixed with sadness? What will they be doing? What will they be thinking about? What will they do without me? Interestingly, these last three questions are the same that freshmen ask, particularly "What will they talk about when I'm not there?" They've been so accustomed to being the center of attention in the family that they're quite certain your life will be a void without them.

There exists a common theme of parents feeling that they were revving their engines for a prophetic departure. A few are surprised at the reaction of their son or daughter. Teena describes her daughter's departure as both of them having been on hold, awaiting the launch for which they had been preparing. As a child, her daughter was one who had chosen to attend camp solo so as not to be tied down. She selected a California college (Seattle was home) where she knew no one and she looked forward to the adventure.

However, even she got homesick for Washington's seasons, layered clothing, smells, and simple and natural life-style habits, all coming as unexpected reminiscences that first year. Teena spoke of feeling much more of an emotional tug when delivering her daughter for the sophomore and junior years. The summers had flown by and there was no ritual of purpose to celebrate the leaving. And Mom knew more clearly how long nine months really were.

Many parents were surprised at their own reaction to the leave taking. From Marianne: "When my son was getting ready, he seemed together and it was just another planning adventure for me. We spent the summer gathering for the harvest, laughing, talking about how great it would be, how excited we all were about his move. We dropped him off at school and on the way home in the car, I fell apart. Totally, relentlessly apart. It hit with no warning—only my husband had expected my reaction and was prepared for it. I was thankful that he took me for a respite first to a park, so reentering my home without my son, the sunshine of my life, would be bearable and forestalled."

In our own lives as parents, we can see it in our own families of origin if the gap in years is large enough. Sally was the first of seven kids who arrived over the course of eighteen years. When she was thirty-six she called her mom on the day that the last sibling had gone off to college only to find her mother weeping. She had been a traditional mom who had made brown-bag lunches for all the kids for more than thirty years. "This is the first day in all these years I have no brown bag to fill," she sighed.

That first day of drop off is often overwhelming. Tom and Donna escorted their daughter, Keri, to the Air Force Academy. The previous flight of young men and women assembled had just departed, and Keri had to stand there alone. Says Dad, "With her little ditty bag at her left side on the ground, she was standing at attention facing west, and thirty-five to forty yards ahead of her and above her was the bridge with the famous line 'Bring Me

Men.' It kind of brought a tear to our eyes. Here's our little Keri standing there at attention and there's the sign that says 'Bring Me Men,' and we brought them a woman."

Where you are taking your freshman can give the trip definition. A Colorado family said, "In 1997 our daughter had the opportunity to attend Stanford in the same class as Chelsea Clinton. The big day arrived and was made even more ceremonious by the president and all the attending hoopla. Stanford handled it very well but still there were reporters lurking. When a reporter started asking my husband and me how we felt about having our daughter attend college with the president's daughter, all we could say was, 'We're too busy with how it feels to have her leave home to worry about anything else.' "

We are all left with questions, many of which make no sense even to us. Why did I encourage her to go away to school? He'll marry an easterner (southerner, westerner, northerner) and never come home. She'll like it so much, she'll never come back. Some have mixed feelings wondering what unexpected help time and distance will provide. And, as always, we change in ways that we would never anticipate.

In cryptic notes are one mother's journal entries for first daughter's ten-and-a-half-hour trip to school: "Whole family plus nearly every possession owned by oldest daughter squeezed into minivan. Drive long, but too short. Laughter, but not like usual. Bouts of sadness. General disquiet. Spend night in motel. Early next morning carry everything into dorm. Unpack. Run to store for essentials. Say good-bye. Hug. Try not to cry. Say good-bye. Hug, try not to cry. Say good-bye. Hug, try not to cry. Say good-bye. Hug, try not to cry. Daughter goes into dorm room and cries. Mother goes into minivan tries not to cry—unsuccessfully." Finds comfort in knowing that she'll talk to Daughter One that evening.

Contrast that with Daughter Two: "One-hour drive to Fort Collins. Convinced two younger sisters they had to drive with parents and could not stay home; Daughter One gone. Daughter Two drives own car. Drive is short. Lots of laughter, teasing. Arrive at college. Finally find place to park. Unload cars and carry everything into dorm. Unpack. No need to buy essentials that we forgot (she will later). Say good-bye. Hug. Daughter Two goes to dorm room and starts her year of socialization. Mother goes to minivan and enjoys remaining daughters, hoping that Daughter Two will call home occasionally." Yet, this is the mother who couldn't say which was more difficult to lose—the first or the second.

One woman recounted, "When my first child left for college, I could not even enter his room at home for two weeks without bursting into tears. When my fourth child left for college, I waved good-bye and immediately cleaned out his closet and placed my clothes there."

There are less traditional departures that nevertheless evoke the full feelings of the rite of passage with its deeper meaning. The ivy-covered towers do not provide the backdrop for all good-byes. Sol's mother wrote about sending him off to Stuntman School in Hollywood. "Well, the day of departure arrived. What can I say except it was hard; in fact, I find my eyes filling with tears once again as I write this. His childhood just went by in a flash and it was incomprehensible how this moment could be here. We tried to keep it quick, said our good-byes, and watched the kids drive off. Gary and I could not speak in fear we'd both start crying. All I know is the phone kept ringing. I guess friends wanted to see how we were doing. I couldn't even talk for three days–I just let the answering machine pick up messages. I remember asking my mother, 'When does the pain go away?' "

While gathering anecdotes from educational consultants, I outlined the book to a man who said, "My leaving was the first time I ever saw my father cry. We weren't even that close and he was crying when they left me at school. I was only three hours away from home."

Again, Donna Damico, reflecting on the recent separation from her son, said, "I've decided these last few months are like the final half hour at work each day. I am a nurse on an acute psychiatric floor and there's never a day that I don't check and double check my worksheet and the medication records as I get ready to leave. As I go down on the elevator, I'm always wondering if there's something I've left undone or forgotten to pass on to the next shift, and checking my pockets to make sure I'm not taking the narcotic keys home with me.

"I have that feeling now, the feeling of unfinished business. Have I left something out of my mothering? How can I squeeze in some last-minute words of wisdom and important anecdotal information about life, and how do I let him know how much I love him? It is time. I've got to believe in the last eighteen years."

We vow to do a good job of parenting from afar and strive to learn our place.

ET, Phone Home

We have been taught to follow their lead, to ask them to let us know what they want. How connected do they wish to stay? What do they wish to tell us about? Our job is to try to stay connected while giving up control. They don't make it easy. We may intellectually understand that requirement, but emotionally it is a pull to be shut out of their transition at the very point when we ourselves are suffering withdrawal.

Marie told wistfully of her only child, Johnny, who went in-state to the University of Southern California. Very close to home. He never called! All the girls' mothers were driving to school, putting up curtains, picking out sheets. Marie says, "I wanted to do that. When I would call, he would say, 'Mom, why are you calling?' " I told him that Steve was calling his mother, that Kelly was calling, and that Kristin was calling . . . . He wanted to know, 'What's all the fuss?' "

Determined and desperate, she tells of having gone to a USC football game just to see him. Her friends said, "Marie, you'll never see him. He's over there in that huge student section." She took binoculars and after a long silent search, handed her friend the binocs and said, "There he is!" She had found him. Connection at last.

When we think of connections, we generally think of the telephone. I didn't want to be a pushy, intrusive mother and played it carefully those first few weeks. I called only on Sundays and checked out to make sure the time would work for him each week. On the third week, he asked me why I didn't call him more often. I told him I thought we had agreed Sundays were the day. He said, "You can call other times. Sunday was just the one we wanted to be sure of."

It is hard to know which works better—knowing how your child is doing or not knowing. One family talked of trying to hold on gently while they watched their son desperately stack up friends his first three months away from home. He made indiscriminate choices, eagerly attaching to the first kids he met without determining whether they had anything in common or whether they could develop a bond to sustain a relationship. When he went back after Christmas break, he realized he had to start all over again—shedding one set of friends and trying to establish another more clearly thought out selection for himself. Others had already found friends and it was rough for him to have to begin all over again socially. He alternated between thinking he'd stay and asking his parents to contact the local university to see if he could transfer. By May he was connected to his new home and his relieved parents could relax a little.

Ray and Sue talked of their daughter: "The firsts were difficult. For Chris they signaled an end, not a beginning. Dorm life was hard. Homesickness was overwhelming. A bout of chicken pox marked the beginning of frequent trips home. Long-distance phone calls added up. Talk of quitting was all too common. But at winter break there was a change. There was more talk about friends at college than high school friends. A visit to her high school produced the comment that it just wasn't the same. Conversations were held about future courses, living off campus, and college activities. At the end of the break, Chris packed the car to go back to college, and pronounced she was ready to go 'home'."

It may be reassuring to think about this transition by considering how they have normally gone through other transitions, such as moving, entering a new school, having friends leave, making new friends, going to camp, graduating from middle school, among other firsts. Even if they do it poorly, you know they'll have their own style and timing and eventually they'll get through it.

Our own expectations color our vision. A mother lamented, "One thing that strikes me is the fact that I wanted my kids to have the wonderful college experience that I had. At Michigan State I was in a sorority, savored the camaraderie, and was caught up in all the fun things that the campus offered. I know now I wanted them to have that experience. I don't know if college has changed, and I suppose sororities come and go. But, I didn't see that happening and it was kind of frustrating. Holly joined a sorority, but it wasn't mine, and I was disappointed. I really wanted to get her in my sorority, but she didn't like it. She didn't like hanging out with the girls. It was just a disappointment that they didn't get involved the way I had. I wanted to relive it, I guess, through them." Others admitted they wished to give their children what they themselves hadn't been able to have.

Repeatedly I listened to parents talk about needing to see the student in the new life. Apparently it works both ways. Shelly's husband gave her a birthday gift to visit her daughter in college. "When I went to visit my daughter for my birthday, it was twenty-eight hours of trying to get a glimpse of her new life. I got a tour of every classroom she had a class in, where she studied in between classes, and even the bathroom she used. She gave wonderful impressions of her teachers lecturing and throwing chalkboards up and down. I met her friends in the dorm and did laundry with her. She kept saying 'Now college is real. You can see what I'm doing.' I knew I needed to see her in her new life but I hadn't realized that she needed me to see her there, too. I realized how much she was missing me when I tried to let her sleep in the next morning, and she said our time together was too short to spend sleeping." In visiting we also get nudges to see our kids as emancipated.

From Judy and Jack: "Another moment of letting go was after a twenty-four-hour visit to the Cornell campus in late September. We watched an intramural soccer game, met his roommate, took them to dinner, breakfast the next morning, and toured campus. As we said good-bye, I took a picture of him walking back to his dorm, savoring the moments he was in sight. I knew that although he enjoyed our visit, he was ready for all the wonderful college experiences ahead. I am grateful for our close relationship and excited for all he will do and become. As I said good-bye, I thought about how the home or grade-school cards were turning into long-distance calls for my birthday, Valentine's Day, and Mother's Day. Although it can tear at my heart at times, I'm okay with it. I have come to realize that we will be needing each other in different ways now. I suppose those needs have been changing continuously since his infancy but having a new home had made it more dramatic."

Another family got a welcome surprise when their son, Jesse, joined the collegiate choir. Despite being in the middle of a fraternity hell week and the accompanying male bonding experiences, he was allowed to suspend his activities so that he could attend his choir performance. His mother writes, "Although he was sleep deprived, semi-starved, and mildly tormented, he showed up at the concert in his tuxedo. He was devastatingly handsome. When the finale came and I got to hear my son sing the Hallelujah Chorus it was a glorious moment for me. It was the best Hanukkah present he could give me."

Having siblings visit the freshmen gives a completely different view. Again, if the college has a sibling weekend and you can afford to send a younger sibling (and if they are wanted), do send them. When our younger son visited his older brother in college for his nineteenth birthday in April, we got a full report consisting of the following pieces of information:

- They have similar time frames—they just go to bed at 4:00 A.M., and sleep until 2:00 P.M.
- Even the cafeterias know—they serve breakfast until 2:30 P.M. When he asked how early they started serving, the answer? "Who knows? Who cares?"
- One boy had added it up. He had eaten four hundred pieces of La Mama's pizza his second semester at school.

- A roommate said on a tired Sunday morning, "I do wish there was someone here to tell me to go to bed!"
- Video games are a large part of college life.

I would have loved the unedited version, although I did ask him to tell me only what he thought I'd want to know. The freshmen may reveal more to siblings, and those confidences present another closed door to the parents.

The open door that is available and that should be utilized is Parents' Weekend. As important as it is for the students, it may be more important to parents. Most colleges provide an opportunity for parents to visit on a sanctioned weekend. That means that you won't have to figure out what to do yourself and you won't make your freshman stand out as the one with unknowing parents. It is simply the best way to be there, feel welcome, and participate. Hope for a later rather than earlier time slot, but go if you can. Most parents admit that it was only after that visit that they were able to settle down and let their child's new life begin.

Our son's Parents' Weekend was shortly into the freshman year and I wish it had been later. On the other hand, I found myself in the laundry room watching a bewildered freshman boy looking questioningly into the washing machine. I smiled and he asked, "Is it okay to wash this in cold?" holding up a clearly favored shirt. "Yes," I said, giving him the rule: Warm for White, Cold for Colors. I felt a part of the dorm and knew Parents' Weekend was a bonus. It is also a time for us to become useful parents.

One friend told of her son's call at the beginning of a Parents' Weekend that they hadn't been able to afford to attend. The boy phoned, crying as he watched the families around him laughing and enjoying one another. He was lonesome and his mother was devastated by the call. She mustered all the courage she could and, without crying, told her very shy son to go outside the door of his dorm, latch onto the first family that went by, and become a part of their family for the weekend. She hung up the phone and cried until she felt she could call back—there was no answer—he had taken her advice and ended up having a wonderful weekend with his adopted family.

Not every family can attend Parents' Weekend and not every freshman has a parent who is available. For parents who do attend, offering to get one more ticket to the game or another seat at the dinner, then nonchalantly including a solo freshman is a good idea. No fuss and no fanfare, however. Just get the tickets, tell them you have an extra, and assume he or she would want to be with you. Take lots of pictures, have great meals, and laugh as much as you can. The good-byes may feel stilted, but know your presence was welcome. No protracted good-byes. Smile, say it has been grand, tell them you can see it will be fine for them, and move on out. If those aren't your exact feelings, find someone else to console you. Your student has all he can deal with at the moment.

It is likely you'll want more contact rather than less after that visit, and e-mail is your solution. If there were ever a time for a parent to get acquainted with the computer, the Internet, and e-mail, it is now. Even as the students become more at home, they continue to use e-mail as their primary communication tool.

If you have e-mail, regardless of where you left off with this parent-freshman relationship, chances are you'll find yourself a recipient. They just can't help themselves.

In the middle of the night when that room looks lonely and unfamiliar, it takes almost no effort to jot down a few words to a parent. It isn't at all like a phone call and feels innocent in the execution. It feels positively wonderful to a parent to sign on and find you have mail from someone who has been a reluctant correspondent. It may be just a few words but they will be treasures. It is also deceptive how much they reveal about your student. Jotting down thoughts and sending them off feels much less revealing, regardless of the content. Printing out and saving the e-mails makes a wonderful log of the college journey.

The e-mails also give you permission to respond and responding in kind is smart. Long, wistful e-mails full of things you wouldn't tell them in person will siphon off your pipeline. At the same time it allows you to be up at 2:30 in the morning, wondering how their life is, knowing you can't call, and just jotting down a few words yourself. "I was up and thinking about you. Hope that test goes well. Love, Mom." It is a touch without intrusion. It also gives you a means of contact if other more traditional means are failing. Shelly said that she e-mailed every day at least once and was surprised when her daughter said, "You never call me." The once weekly phone calls weren't enough and e-mail isn't always the same.

One freshman e-mailed sending a joke a day to fifty people but didn't call her parents. Being on the joke list was their contact. Better than nothing, that's for sure.

Meanwhile Back
at the Ranch

For those far away, Thanksgiving is usually the first visit home. It is eagerly anticipated by the freshmen. Expectation is high and emotions are everywhere. When my son returned the Wednesday before Thanksgiving, he was like a puppy sniffing every room to find the familiar, comforting scents. After an hour or so of confirming his space . . . now what to do? There we were ready to talk, play cards, watch TV, even go somewhere or just listen. He had started pacing. He didn't know what to do with himself. Not exactly a caged animal but a confused one–liking the reacquaintance with familiar surroundings yet missing the routine of the dorm. I was fighting off trying to fix it when he started dialing. No one else home yet and the dissonance remained until he received a compatriot's call.

Luckily we had decided to share Thanksgiving with knowing friends whose daughter was a high school senior. When we got there, relief spread over his body. A kindred soul. Although I wish he had been as excited to be with us, I was grateful to have a loving Thanksgiving where he could enjoy both worlds. It was then that it became clear that he had made a shift. He asked hesitatingly, fearfully, hopefully–"Do you think I've changed?" Wondering himself whether he had changed and if so how, and whether for the better, and what better was. There was happiness in my heart that he had begun to find a new home and longing in my soul that I was only a minor part of it.

The aftermath of vacations is particularly informative. "When my daughter went back to school after Christmas," one mother wrote, "I was surprised at how sad I felt. The lump in my throat was huge and my stomach ached. When I went to do volunteer work at my younger daughter's school library, I thought I was fine until the librarian asked me how I was. I burst into tears and said, 'I'm not doing well at all. My daughter went back to school yesterday and I feel so silly for missing her so much.' This mother of older children said to me in such a sweet way. 'That's not silly and it never goes away.' That reassures me somehow. Another woman I know sent her last child to school this year and said she wasn't prepared for how quiet it was now. "When your children go away to school, their friends do, too."

Mother Nature pushes us along. Spring break is the first extended time off with little family demands. Some students flock home. Others have made connections at school and venture off into worlds their parents aren't a part of. If you were expecting your freshman to come home for every vacation, the first absence is a symbolic announcement. If it happens during the freshman year, the jolt may help you get ready for the summer return.

Some complain of the shock when kids return for the summer—clothes strewn everywhere, nocturnal living habits. Others welcome the activity.

Barbara's solution: "In anticipation of the invasion of the four kids home from college, I decided that I would establish rules to make this summer better than last. For hours I kept trying to have a meeting with all four only to have the phone ring, some friend stop over, some interruption to my most important meeting. Finally I lost my cool and ordered all four big college kids to the car. They thought I had lost my mind, but we all sat in the car with the windows up, no phone, no music, and had the meeting I felt necessary for sanity. I gave the rules:

- I don't care where you keep your clothes—in your car, under your bed, in a friend's garage, but I will not have anything on the floor in any room in my house. Anything I see will go immediately to Goodwill.

- If you are going to be out late, I want to know early so I am not worried that something horrible has happened to you. When you come home you are to check on the other kids—the last one home turns all the lights out, before that all the lights stay on so that I can determine quickly when all four kids are home. Also, you are to remember that we go to work around here and cannot be up all night.

- We have a washer and dryer for your use. My advice is to keep your clothes separate from everyone else's and don't think that if you leave a load of wash in the washing machine and go out that it is miraculously going to jump into the dryer. The rest of us have our own lives, so pay attention to your own things.

- If you are going to be home for dinner, great. If you are not going to be home for dinner, please tell us ahead. I'm finding I cook one night and no one is home, the next night I don't cook and everyone appears home for dinner. We need to communicate.

It worked. While no one was happy about sitting in the car for the meeting, they understood it was going to be difficult for six adults who were used to living alone to all of a sudden be back in the same home. I should have had meetings in the car for all those high school years. By the way, Goodwill did make a killing the first week or two, and then nothing."

Another parent, Diana, said that when her son and daughter came home that first summer after the freshman year, she felt as if she were a mom with three kids in the sandbox. "I was the Mom, and Dad was playing with the kids."

One friend talked about when her first child left for college: "I counted every day before as practically a death-sentence countdown. Years later, when all four kids would come home from college for the summer or Christmas break, I quietly counted the days until they would leave. My love for the children had not changed, just my life!"

Another mother said she realized that every time they came back, they had come back changed. More of who they were going to be. "But, the kids didn't understand that we were changing, too. They expected to come back to Ozzie and Harriet's house." And, to be honest, our kids change in ways we least expect. My son, who had never done laundry in his life, came home folding his shirts as if he were working at Abercrombie & Fitch.

Just as they get used to their new lives, we get used to ours. Our task is to blend the changes in both. We begin to be more respectful of differences, and hope that by our example we are given the same gift from them.

Will the Circle
Be Unbroken ?

In addition to adjusting to their changing world while trying to find our place in it, and adjusting to our own new life and discovering their place in it, we find ourselves discovering our new life with only a hint of their presence. At first we notice their absence in surprising moments: buying fewer groceries, noticing how less often the water softener demands attention; having the ice machine ready and able; finding the car radio station unchanged and gas in the car; and having the garage door shut, the alarm system turned on, the phone relatively quiet, the answering machine empty, the shampoo bottle not almost empty, less laundry, mourning animals, food in the refrigerator, and the scissors where they belong.

My friend Cheri said, "Dan and I were on our own! It sure was quiet around the house. The basement was dark. No kids coming and going at all hours. We could come and go as we pleased. Fewer groceries to buy, fewer clothes to wash, no phones ringing at all hours. No ball games to attend. Empty Nesters at last!

"We are slowly adjusting. Dan or I talk to Scott at least every other day. He has had a great first semester. He pledged a fraternity, made lots of new friends, has a girlfriend, plays football and basketball for his fraternity, and even got good grades! What more could we ask for? How about a few hours a day with him to discuss the day, his plans and his dreams? How about a few more ball games to watch him play? How about attending church on Sunday with him and going to brunch afterwards?"

In our adjusting we sometimes feel guilt. Our son went to visit his brother at college and my husband and I went on a trip alone. At first it felt like a betrayal when we rented a two-door convertible and stayed at a bed and breakfast in a small, quaint, quiet ocean town that would have bored the kids.

Almost shamefully, Susan told of being relieved to be able to help her eighth grader with no distractions. The continued flurry of activity the previous year had been both entertaining and consuming. It was peaceful to be able to spend an uninterrupted stretch with a struggling, quiet fourteen-year old. On one level, no competition felt fine to him.

Yet, siblings often long for the old relationship. While we are floundering in our own adjustment, it is easy to overlook the loss felt by the sibling left at home. He, too, feels the empty nest. Our introverted Mike swore he'd be in heaven when more extroverted John had finally left. It took him only minutes to take over the room and make it his own. For the first few weeks when asked if he missed John, he adamantly said, "No. What's to miss–he was mean to me." But, when he was waiting for the day to come that John would be back with all the activity, I overheard Mike say to the kids in the carpool: "Boy, I can't wait for John to get home. I'll finally have something to listen to." Each time, though, that anticipation led to disappointment in part because it could never be as wonderful as he had wished and because some things never change. Nevertheless, each visit brought hope.

And, ultimately, it became clear that John had brought a great deal of activity to our home. My husband noted how quiet the house was now "You take only one fourth out but the circle feels broken, not just smaller. Or are there now two circles that you hope will intersect often? You try the first few weeks to function normally. Work is the same, but you know things have changed irretrievably."

After each departure Mike noticed the lull. His conclusion was that his parents were the lacking agent. One night, when we were discussing other problems, he told us that his "real" parents were quite different. Their names were Chris and Linda, were thirty-five years old, and lived in Florida. All of our flaws were missing in them. In fact, he had posted a drawing of them on his bulletin board, I suppose, to remind him of more exciting times elsewhere. That was his solution to his sag in spirit.

Families find out much about themselves with the departure of a special child. One bewildered father, Roger, realizing his wife's sorrow and his fourteen-year-old son's grieving, decided to drive farther north to see his mother after dropping his daughter off at college. How could he? How could he misjudge his wife's feelings? Perhaps he thought it would make his wife feel better, or at least he had thought he'd take his wife to someone with whom he associated caregiving and comfort for himself. His wife was enraged; he was blindsided; she got even more angry when he didn't understand. She had just lost the firstborn, her soul mate. She wanted to go home and be alone to grieve.

Parents admit that the activities of childhood keep the heartbeat of a family going. One mom recounted the starkness of life without their daughter. She saw her husband in a new, overly bleak light and felt an unfillable hollow hole in their family. At first it seemed potentially fatal. To pour all our feelings into one loss when losses are actually cumulative and represent many transitions over time is risky. It is hard to comprehend the tapestry of loss, but identifying what you are grieving for helps.

Our hopes become apparent. We hope our children find a passion. We hope they have as much fun as we had. We hope they have it better than we had it. We hope that they know it is okay if they make choices that would not be our choices. Your friends become divided into two groups: those who understand and those who do not. We enjoy the tender words of those who know we feel both joy and despair. For a short time nothing else seems to matter. Then the sun shines again and we begin to make our life circumstance fit the reality.

What we continue to hear is that by May of the freshman year, many mothers in particular begin to feel as though they have let go. They know the students are coming home and, although they are excited to see them, things are different. Many say that even when parents visit kids at college they can't get the feeling back. Then, slowly, a parent realizes he or she is no longer that part of their lives. Instead, parents have new parts in their children's lives, more as peers than as parents. They have to be content with knowing they've done their part.

One father commented that he tended to call his own parents more often, now knowing they must have missed the contact, too. He remembered that he thought his own leaving had had no impact on them.

A mother of several children whose oldest son left for college said she missed him miserably but talked about how nice it was getting to know her younger children in a new way. Echoing her sentiments, a friend said, "I am really appreciating this. As much as I miss my daughter, I am enjoying the younger kids. They seem instantly older. Firstborn children are so new in everything they do that they get lots of the family's attention. They are the practice kids. The younger ones may not have had the same amount of attention but now they benefit because I know how short their time at home is. I appreciate every minute they are willing to give me.

"The challenge for us now is what we call 'the comings and goings.' My daughter feels like she is never all in one place. When she comes home, things are different. Life has gone on and younger siblings are older. I want to grab every second with her that I can and put regular life on hold. We all act like she is visiting and this feels awful. Her routine is at school. Her being gone has left such a big hole that we have filled it up by turning to each other and she feels left out. I wonder how other families handle this?"

Some parents discover their importance in ways they'd never guess. From a flight attendant: "We fly each month with different women and in that jump seat we talk about the most intimate details of our lives. In jump seat therapy," she continues, "we talk about women valuing their child-rearing role." Yes, there and everywhere is validation of that job which we experience when they leave. It becomes apparent that our job has been a meaningful one. At the same time it is frightfully predictable that a woman looks at her husband and discovers that the children have filled her life and that she needs to get to know him once again. Many women talk about moving or redecorating once the kids are gone, as if to fill their time better. Others want to get rid of large houses and go smaller to punctuate the transition.

After that last child leaves, for many parents the bottom drops out of their heart. Women see all the time spent on kids and realize they've got some work ahead of them. There is also a feeling that women believe men aren't as "full" from children and thus feel the loss less. One comment was, "Women have different space in their hearts." It would appear that caregiving fills their hearts.

As we come to the end of this longest journey, we find that our own lives have a curious parallel to our children's lives. We are both in transition, starting a new life. It is a time of reflection for parents to look back over where they've recently been, to take its measure, to review its lessons, and to recognize that we are on the other side of the passage.

In the end, stories are what's left of us: we are no more than the few tales that persist.

⤳ Salman Rushdie

Home
Remedies

- Write a real letter.
- Send great gossipy letters to your child about high school news, sports, hometown trivia.
- Save the e-mails and bind them for that graduation party.
- Buy clear plastic containers to store their things in–so it doesn't look discarded, only saved.
- Make that first birthday (or holiday) away from home a fine one.
- Be prepared to hate seeing their room so clean.
- Go to Parents' Weekend if at all possible.
- If there's a student whose parents have been unable to attend Parents' Weekend, be a substitute parent.
- Send a sibling to Sibling Weekend if possible.
- Introduce yourself to residence hall advisors who

have your best interest at heart.

- Get a(nother) dog if you miss your previously noisy, lively house.

- If your dog misses your freshman, give the dog an old shoe or some other reminder.

- Making and sending care packages that are really personal can be so much fun. Like playing Santa.

- Be pleasant and pliable.

- Pare down and omit all but the essential.

- Take care of marital problems in private. On the other hand, don't let students be surprised by major family crises.

- Talk in springtime about the summer—what you're expecting when your child comes home—hours, jobs, car, money (getting, spending, and saving).

- Know your limits and what battles are truly worth it. (Most aren't.)

- Chronicle good events.

- Minimize bad news.

- Remember: Hinting is always transparent.

- Put together all those photos at last.

- Smell their clothes regularly—don't clean it all. No sanitizing.

- Continue old traditions with siblings still at home. Also, find ways to celebrate their newly found slots.

- Don't believe all you hear.

- Read the student handbooks so you know the options.

- Stay away from parents whose kids are perfect.

- Call your own parents.

176

- Laugh more.
- Plant something whose growth parallels these times.
- Find a way to become involved yourself.
- Trust that they're already much of what they'll be.
- Say "I love you" often.

Farewell

he robust journey these past months has been filled to overflowing with emotions and experiences for the students and for the parents. Last time for this, first time for that, good-byes and hellos, successes and failures, closed doors and open gates, the seriousness and the absurdity, the calm winds and the stormy seas. In fact, looking back, it feels like the turning of the weathervane in Mary Poppins, signaling the time for her to move on. The hope is that, as we near the end of this voyage and await their first summer home, we can rejoice in the passage. We trust that relationships have not only survived but have become enriched along the way. Though the nest is empty, our heart is full.

It is time. Our cherished children are now embraced by a new family. We need to trust that our values carry from home to school. It is also our hope that their new world confirms and even broadens their validity.

There have been many lessons we've discovered along our journey. We learned to know when to listen and when to speak, when to do and when to wait, realizing that we will be needing each other in different ways now. Knowing all of this gives us the confidence we need to acknowledge life's affirmations as well as its mysteries.

As the circle of life repeats, we would wish to be blessed with each of us growing into a new, fuller person and with a family in which the whole is greater than the sum of its parts.

And so to begin . . .

May you find a way to fill your time with something that fills your heart.

-℮ Teena Barnett, JST

CHILDREN

Your children are not your children.
They are the sons and daughters of
life's longing for itself.

They come through you but not from you,
and though they are with you
yet they belong not to you.

You may give them your love,
but not your thoughts,
for they have their own thoughts.

You may house their bodies
but not their souls,
for their souls dwell in the house of tomorrow,
which you cannot visit
not even in your dreams.

You may strive to be like them,
but seek not to make them like you.

For life goes not backward
nor tarries with yesterday.

You are the bows from which your children
as living arrows are sent forth.

The archer seeks the mark
upon the path of the infinite,
and He bends you with his might that his arrows may
go swift and far.

Let your bending in the
archer's hand be for gladness:

For even as he loves the arrow that flies,
so he loves also the bow that is stable.

Kahlil Gibran

Acknowledgments

I am grateful to many who helped with this book. My thanks go to Andrea Peabbles for her thoughtful, thorough editing. I am indebted to Mary Beth Starzel, long time friend, soulmate and wizard of words, whose enthusiasm and sparkle are threaded throughout the book. Mark Sklarow remained a faithful cheerleader and was more important than he can ever know. I am especially thankful to Donna Damico and Charlie Mayer for being trailblazers and for Johanna Parker's artwork whose magic matches her tender spirit.

I can never repay Jean Marie Martini and Harriett Graves for enduring this innocent project. Jean Marie's tenacity, soulful and spirited contributions, her *we can fix it* flexibility, combined with good New England common sense, were vital and simply wonderful. Harriett's unflagging commitment to finding a way to do things right and her meticulous, warm, encouraging, trustworthy, good-natured, steady hand guided this journey. Thanks to both Harriett and Jean Marie who spent endless hours in the upstairs salon, calling, researching, talking, laughing, and being kind to Bernie whose tail frequently whisked away our work. I thank my family, who not only rose above the chaos, but who also allowed me the freedom to write about our own journey. My cup runneth over.

I also wish to
thank the following friends,
counselors, advisors, magic helpers
and good Samaritans for graciously
sharing their journeys and
for illuminating our path.

Sally Aderton

Teena Barnett

Jan Becher

Ray and Sue Bodis

Carla & Daryl Carlson

Carol Charles

Bo & Lynn Cottrell

Donna Damico

Kyle Davenport

Eileen Doida

Taylor Dufford

Robert A. Elliott

Judy Fallin

Gene Farrell

Madonna Ferguson

Donna & Tom Fox

Barbara & Bill Goldy

Ellen Goodman

Pete & Suzanne Guy

Rusty Haynes

Nick Kamau

Cynthia & Lloyd Kull

Dan & Cheri Issel

Father William P. Leahy

Gary & Elise Lubell

Sarah Myers McGinty

Steve & Susie Mostow

John & DeAnne Olsen

Doris Olson

Mary Parman

John & Marie Perrone

Jack & Judy Pottle

Irene Rawlings

John & Martha Richards

Pat & Jayne Russell

Curt & Diana Rummel

Gary & Judy Saltzman

Donna Savage

Charles "Red" Scott

Jordan Silver

Ken & Judy Simon

Nolan & Dianne Singleton

Mark Sklarow

Chip & Dorothy Sommers

Lynn & LeAnn Southam

Ginny Tice

Marie Vachon

John & Susie Wagner

Bruce & Shelly Wilhelm

Rhea Wolfram

Resources

Clary, Deborah, *College Survival Handbook*
Andrews & McNeel, 1997.

Cormier, Robert, *Eight Plus One*
Laurel-Leaf Books, 1980.

Gibran, Kahlil, *The Prophet*
Alfred A Knopf, Inc., 1923.

MacGowan, Sandra F. and Sarah M. McGinty,
College Admission Directors Speak to Parents
Harcourt Brace Jovanovich, 1988.

McGinty, Sarah Myers, *The College Application Essay*
College Board, 1997.

O'Brien, George Dennis, *What to Expect from College:
University President's Guide for Students and Parents*
New York: St. Martin's Press, 1991.

Shunk, Rusty, *A Funny Thing Happened on the Way to
the Admissions Office*, National Association of College
Admissions Counseling, 1995.

Steinberg, Laurence, *Crossing Paths*
Sasquatch Books, 1997.

College Freshman Survival Guide Videotape
Octameron Associates, POB 2748, Alexandria, VA
22301; 703/836-5480;   Fax 703/836-5650.

Order form

- FAX ORDERS   303 671-5200
- TELEPHONE ORDERS   Call Toll Free: 1-877-231-1234
  Please have Visa or MasterCard ready
- ON-LINE ORDERS   anerus2@aol.com
- POSTAL ORDERS   Simpler Life Press
  222 Milwaukee, Suite 403
  Denver, CO 80206
- TELEPHONE   303 377-1486

Please send me the following books

____*Empty Nest...Full Heart*
    The Journey from Home to College $14.95

____*A Woman's Guide to a Simpler Life* . . $14.00

____*Lifelines: A Personal Journal* $12.95

Company Name   _____

Name   _____

Address   _____

City _____State _____Zip _____

Telephone (____)_____

SALES TAX

Please add 3.8% for books shipped to Colorado address

SHIPPING

$4.00 for the first book and $2.00 for each additional book

                           Total Payment _____

_____Check

_____Credit card: ____Visa   ____Master Card

Card Number _____

Name on Card: _____

           Exp. Date   ____/ ____

Signature _____

CALL TOLL FREE AND ORDER NOW!
1-877-231-1234

About the author...

Andrea Van Steenhouse, Ph.D., is a psychologist in
private practice in Colorado. Following a twelve-year
career in radio as a talk show host, Andrea continues to
make frequent appearances as a highly visible expert on
matters of the heart, soul, and life passages. She lives
in Denver with her husband and sons.